Laughter Calls Me

Laughter Calls Me

Catherine Brown

Lighthouse Trails Publishing
Silverton, Oregon U.S.A.

LAUGHTER CALLS ME

©2003, 2006 by Catherine Brown
Second Edition, Softbound

Lighthouse Trails Publishing Company
P.O. Box 958
Silverton, Oregon 97381
editor@lighthousetrails.com
www.lighthousetrails.com

Scripture quotations are taken from the *King James Version* and the *New King James Version*. Copyright for NKJV ©1982 by Thomas Nelson, Inc. Used by permission. All rights reserved.

"annie died the other day." Copyright©1961, 1989, 1991 by the Trustees for the E.E. Cummings Trust, from COMPLETE POEMS: 1904 - 1962 by E.E. Cummings, edited by George J. Firmage. Used by permission of: Liveright Publishing Corporation.

All other poems by Catherine Brown ©2003

Special thanks to Robert Savannah,
U. S. Fish and Wildlife Service for use of linedrawing (p.80).
Other lineart drawings by "Shannan."
Drawing on Dedication page from Harpers [Public Domain]
Cover Photo by "Shannan."
Cover Design by Catherine Brown and Kathy Campbell

Library of Congress Cataloging-in-Publication Data

Brown, Catherine, 1954-
    Laughter calls me / Catherine Brown. — 2nd ed.
        p. cm.
    ISBN 0-9721512-6-5 (softbound : alk. paper)
    1. Child abuse. 2. Abused children. 3. Brown, Catherine, 1954- I.
Title.
HV6626.5.B77 2006
362.76'3'092—dc22

                                        2005009327

Printed in the United States of America

To my children
Without whom
Laughter never would have called

Acknowledgments

I first want to thank David Dombrowski, my editor and publisher, for believing in this book. And a special thanks to the district attorney of our fair community—though I cannot mention your name, you deserve recognition for believing the kids and devoting your life to justice. To the LAPD and former FBI Special Agent Roger Young, thank you for being there for so many children. I also cannot leave out my deep gratitude to my mother and dad—your love and support carried us through. And above all thank you to my children who gave me permission to tell our story and a special hug and thank you to Ben for your support and encouragement. It meant more to me than you can know.

*****

Some of the names and places in this story have been changed in order to protect the innocent.

*****

All of the facts in this story have been verified with police reports, trial transcripts, psychiatric reports and other documents.

*****

Warning

Parts of this account are not suitable for children. We have allowed the author freedom in her story (with some restraint), as we know there are still people in the world today who think these things do not happen. This is a story that testifies of the truth with the hope that bringing light into darkness will dispel the darkness.

An Important Note From The Publisher

L aughter Calls Me is a true account. It covers a fifteen year span of time, from a young girl's search for truth during the hippie revolution of the '60s and '70s to a world so deviant and shocking you may have trouble reading some parts. But it is a rare book because in the midst of this tragic story is a growing thread of hope and joy.

As you read through this novel-like story, you will be taken into the author's search, and you will feel with her the fears and frustrations of searching for truth in a world full of falsehood and danger. But the book does not end with her discovery of truth but delves into the pursuing years as the author is struck with the cruelest of blows and a second discovery that could potentially destroy her and her children.

For a moment, as you are carried from her first discovery to the next, you may wonder if you have not indeed begun to read a second book until you realize her initial discovery is the foundation for what lies ahead. This change of flow may be likened to a mighty stream suddenly bursting upon a large boulder, reorienting itself on another path. In that stream the water preceding the boulder is what pushes on and keeps the stream flowing.

In this young woman's quest and through the devastating results of her own miscalculations, she also finds the wonder and joy in motherhood to the bravest children of all. We will peer out with her from her window as she watches her children laughing and playing. She is reminded that even through the darkest times, God is with us, and we can walk in joy with Him, not because of the darkness and evil that happens to us, but because He has gone before us preparing the way; it is sometimes through the greatest pain that the greatest joy is birthed. Let us go now to where her search begins and where it ultimately leads her…

Contents

Laughter Calls Me

Laughter calls me to its side,
I really don't know why.
It's dark and cold outside;
Nothing has gone right,
Everything is wrong.
Isn't it what I see that really matters?

My children dance and giggle and play.
Life whispers to them, "Let's go."
Willingly they follow.
They don't know that we are poor,
That life is hard.
To them, I am their queen,
They are my princes and princesses.
Laughter calls me to its side.
I really wonder why.

Spring is coming,
Winter never lasts forever.
I watch the children, through the open window,
Beckoning me—
"Come mama and play, the sun is shining."
I dry my tears,
And run to meet their outstretched arms...
Running through the fields of daisies in my mind;
That's good enough for me.
Laughter calls me to its side
Now, I know why.

Catherine Brown

One

Imagine There's No God

"Hey man, try this." A classmate handed me a funny looking cigarette. "It will make you feel better than you ever have before."
"What is it?" I asked.

"Hey man, it's weed, you know, marijuana." I ran excitedly over to my friend's house and showed her the odd smelling cigarette. We snuck down to the creek's edge, making sure no one was around then shared what was to change our lives instantly. I was fifteen years old and knew somehow I had crossed a line. There was no turning back.

Almost overnight, I changed from a shy, top-grade student to a longhaired, barefoot hippie. When I was high, it seemed like the whole universe opened before me, and as I began experimenting with heavier drugs, I really believed they were leading me closer and closer to truth.

The year was 1970, and a revolution of young people tore at the very foundation of our country. Boldly denouncing the conventional lifestyles we had known as children, we grew our hair long, put on beads, flowers, holey jeans and funky dresses, and dropped out of society as we perceived it. Hunting zealously for some other meaning to life, we vehemently condemned government, materialism and capitalism.

I first sensed an emptiness in my heart at the age of ten.

Often, I sat alone in a secluded corner of our suburban backyard and gazed into the California sky, searching for some sign from outer space. Later at twelve, I began wondering if a God had created mankind and if we had a reason for being here on this planet. On Saturday afternoons, I hopped on my red bicycle and headed for the rolling foothills that surrounded our town. Spending hours wading through the creeks, tossing rocks and catching frogs, I'd then lay on top of the grassy hills and watch the cloud-filled sky. I was fascinated with its apparent eternity.

At fourteen, I met some kids at school who were Mormons and started attending their church, thinking, *perhaps they have the answer to this void I feel.* However, after six months of early morning seminary about a man named Joseph who saw angels and visions, I felt disappointed and unfulfilled.

Thus I began my fifteenth year, feeling lost and confused. My mom and dad didn't know what to do when they saw their daughter changing. My outrageous clothing matched with long, stringy hair became a major sore spot between us. My grades plummeted as I lost interest in the *unimportant* things of life. When my friends changed from clean-cut, well-behaved kids to long-haired, starry-eyed ones, my parents became terrified.

One night, after my exasperated father told me to stop hanging around my new pals or else, I climbed out my bedroom window, taking only the clothes on my back. Without looking back, I took off running—destination unknown.

The following afternoon, somewhere between San Francisco and Reno, Nevada, the police pulled up beside me as I stood hitchhiking on the side of a bustling California highway. "Can I please see your I.D.?" the officer requested.

"I don't have any," I stated truthfully.

"How old are you?" he questioned, looking at me intently.

"Eighteen," I lied.

"Well then, it's illegal for you to walk around without identification." I murmured something about never hearing of that law before and wondered if I could possibly look older than my fifteen years. "What's your name?" he asked.

"Mary," I lied again.

"Mary what?" he questioned. My not-so-well-thought-out intention was to say Mary Taylor, an actual family ancestor of ours, but instead I stumbled, saying,

"Mary Tyler."

"Oh, and I suppose you're going to say Mary Tyler Moore next," he laughed. I stood dumbfounded for having said such a brainless thing. From then on it was all downhill. The officer transported me to the nearest juvenile hall, a detestable and grim place. As another officer led me through a drab-green day room past the female *residents*, fifty pairs of hard, angry eyes pierced me. Adorned with heavy eyeliner and ratted hair, they appeared to be unbreakable in spirit. I couldn't help wonder what tragedies had befallen them. How had they become so lifeless yet so full of living rage? Were they scared? They didn't act it.

At the prospect of spending countless days there, I gave the officer my name and phone number. Mom and Dad arrived a few hours later, relieved their runaway girl hadn't been murdered and thrown to the side of some highway. They threw their arms around me then took me home.

Though drugs obliterated my interest in school, I graduated in 1972. A few days after graduation, when caps and gowns had barely been put away, I zealously announced my new plans—"I'm moving to Canada to live off the land." Reading Brad Angier's book, *How to Live in the Woods on Pennies a Day*, proved just the inspiration I needed. With an old, second-hand army backpack loaded to the brim with essential items, I bought a Greyhound bus ticket to Vancouver, B.C., Canada, the town of my birth and the first eight years of my life.

My grandparents met me at the bus depot in Vancouver and took me to their stucco, cottage-style house on the outskirts of the city. Granny was an English woman, who served tea with cream and sugar each evening along with delicate homemade pastries. She was a tall, delightful woman whose contagious laugh permeated off the walls of her home, making everyone around her happy—the children most of all.

Grandad was a true Welshman, quiet and soft-spoken. He had been employed with Vancouver's city hospital for over thirty years as their painter. Day after day, he went from one end of the building to the other, meticulously painting the snow-white walls over and over. He often fished in the ocean and brought home large salmon for granny to can, which she did carefully and successfully. Lunches in the summer consisted of salmon on homemade white bread, creamy butter and cups of hot steaming tea, made only as an English grandmother can do.

Maybe I loved my grandparents so much because they saw the good in everything and everyone. "You're a good girl, honey," Granny said as they reluctantly drove me to the old northbound highway. No matter what crazy, youthful ideas her hippie grandchildren conjured up, she always told us how wonderful we were and without a doubt knew we would turn out *just fine*.

Now standing alone on a highway that led to the Alberta Peace

The highway in British Columbia I was traveling on

River country, my heart beat fast with anticipation, and yes, with fear. I held out my shaky hand, extended my thumb, and could think of nothing else at that moment but the risks involved in hitchhiking. A girl all alone, heading into the wilds of North America, surely becomes prey to all kinds of peril.

After two short rides, which took me an insignificant fifty miles, a suave, city man in a Lincoln Continental pulled over and offered me a ride. We rode along for hours, stopping only for food, coffee and gasoline. By three in the afternoon, we were high up in the mountains and my *chauffeur* started drinking. As he finished his second beer, his already fast driving shifted to erratic racing, and I thought for sure we would drive right over the edge of the steep, unrailed cliffs. Eventually, the windy road straightened out, and I breathed a long sigh of relief. *Ah*, I thought, resting my head against the window, *maybe this hitchhiking isn't going to be so bad after all.* I was a strong-willed girl and hated to think I couldn't do something just because I was female.

As dusk approached, and without any warning at all, this guy, who by then had guzzled several beers, reached over and grabbed me. I screamed and slapped his hand away.

"Hey what's the problem?" he laughed. "Don't you want to have a little fun? After all, what are you doing out here hitchhiking alone if you aren't looking for a good time?"

"Stop this car, and let me out right now!" I ordered. I could hear a tremble in my voice and hoped *he* could not. Mumbling under his breath angry words I could not understand, he slammed on his brakes while I grabbed my heavy pack and jumped out of the car. He peeled out, leaving me alone on a deserted, mountain road hundreds of miles from anyone. With darkness imminent, I sat down on a rock and cried. *All of my big ideas—here it is, my first day and all that matters now is home.* I was hungry, cold and frightened. Suddenly all I wanted was to be home where it was safe. *If I am going to do this living-in-the-woods thing, I'm going to have to get a job and buy a car.* That night, I slept in some bushes by the side of the road and in the morning walked to the nearest town, caught a bus and went back to California. My short-lived plan to live off the land came to a screeching halt.

Once home, I found an apartment near the city of Oakland and a job as a nurse's aide in a convalescent hospital. Through a college newspaper I found a girl named Julie who needed a roommate. Right away she moved in with me. We each worked during the weekdays and got high on the weekends. Julie had a steady boyfriend, but I went from one failed relationship to another.

Sometimes I smoked pot, but mostly I dropped LSD. For me, psychedelic drugs had become an integral part of my life, offering an escape from the turmoil within, the turmoil I couldn't seem to ignore any other way.

I believed LSD reached into the untouched realms of my mind. During acid trips, I sensed there was a God and thought by getting high I might actually see Him.

One night, Julie and I went to a party we'd been invited to. The event was in a gigantic, ominous-looking old house with large windows and shades pulled tightly closed. When we arrived, many people we'd never seen before were heading into an underground root cellar. Once inside the cellar, I struggled to see as dimly lit strobe lights flickered multi-colored beams in every direction. The smoke was so thick breathing became difficult. A rowdy band played songs by the Rolling Stones, and the large room was packed. After we'd been there a few minutes, Julie came up to me and handed me four, little blue tablets. "Here," she said smiling. "Take these." I popped them all in my mouth, swallowing hard. As I started to feel the effects of the drug, not even knowing what it was, an obnoxious boy asked me to dance.

"No thanks," I said. He grabbed my arm anyway and began tugging me to the dance floor. As I pulled back, a voice came from behind.

"Leave her alone." It was Julie, to the rescue. She was laughing and having a great time. At that moment, I wished I was more like her—free and outgoing. Instead, I was shy and insecure.

As Julie made her way back into the crowd, I realized the little blue tablets I took were very potent. Soon, the room began to sway as my feet teetered unsteadily. The band played a song, something about a stupid girl, and I wondered if they were singing about me. Paranoid thoughts filled my head as it became harder to breathe. Julie introduced me to an old East Indian man whose long, black hair hid most of his brown, wrinkled face and whose smile revealed stained, misshapen teeth. *Some kind of happy guru,* I guessed. They laughed while heading for the dance floor.

I worked my way through the crowd of moving, colorful people and climbed the rickety, wooden stairs that led outdoors. Motion and color were intensified; even the music did not sound like music anymore, just loud, vulgar shouting. A lot of commotion was going on outside as a rowdy group of Harley Davidson bikers arrived on the scene. Someone said something about a fight. Minutes later, three police cars showed up, and I didn't doubt there was going to be trouble.

I stood in the middle of the driveway away from the fast growing mob. Suddenly, to my surprise, I saw Julie walking away from the root cellar towards the street. She was laughing and waving good-bye to me. Flanked on each side of her strode two men I'd never seen before, and walking behind the three of them glided the happy guru. They rounded the corner and disappeared into the darkness. I raced down the long, gravel driveway and stood on the edge of the road, looking but seeing no one. *Maybe those guys have taken her against her will,* I thought. *She could be in danger. I have to find her, have to help her.*

So, into the darkness I ran, running through the city to find my friend, who I was sure had just been kidnapped. Walking and sometimes running for what seemed like hours, still high from the drug, I wondered why the effects were lasting so long. As I passed people on the street, they seemed to be staring at me, almost incredulously. *What's wrong with these people? Why are they staring? Surely, they aren't in on this too!* Running down the street, I became more concerned about escaping the people than about finding Julie. Fear, anxiety, dread, paranoia—the feelings none of us talked about when we were straight, but they were very real.

Hoping to escape the gawking stares of these *hostile* strangers, I found my way to a side street in which dim streetlights softly displayed quaint, little shops and stores. In the daytime this place, no doubt, pervaded with bustling activity but now sat empty. *Those people, why were they staring? Is it my hair, my clothes?* I stopped to catch my reflection in one of the shop windows and gasped in horror at what I saw. It wasn't I but an old withered woman ... dressed like me! Her face was wrinkled like a raisin, and she was bent over as if in agony. *This, this isn't me,* I frantically told myself. Touching my face with cold, sweating hands, all I could feel were deep creases and furrows. *My God, something terrible is happening. I'm turning into an old woman.* I began running, afraid to look any longer.

Distraught, I tried finding my way back to our apartment but to no avail. I was lost and had no idea where I was. I had heard stories of those who took drugs laced with poisons, and they never came off the high; they just went totally crazy, never returning to normal. My mind drifted to the image of a longhaired man I had seen in a hospital once. He was about twenty-five, and as he sat on a couch, his eyes stared with a blank look. I searched for some sign of life, some hint of acknowledgment. Except for the inhaling, exhaling movements of his chest, he showed no indication of life. They said he'd taken LSD one day and had been like that ever since.

Running down the barely lit street, looking more like a savage animal than a young girl, my eyes were wild with fear, my hair loose and damp with sweat. I noticed something going on down the street. Cautiously, I approached and saw two police officers searching the premises of a yard. Their silhouettes stood out under the dim street lights. "Can you help me?" I cried out. They walked towards me and called out,

"What's wrong?"

"I think my roommate has been kidnapped from this party."

"Where's the party?" one of them asked as they now stood in front of me. My lips closed tightly, certain their intentions were to raid the party and arrest everyone. "We can't help unless you tell us," the officer spoke in a stern voice. I began to panic, not wanting them to leave. I was afraid by now I would end up like that guy in the hospital. As they turned to go, I cried out, "I think I'm having a bad trip." Stopping and turning, they gazed intently at me. Their voices softened, "I think it would be a good idea if we took you up to the hospital." It didn't take much to convince me to go along. Not sure whether I was overdosing or not, they rushed me to the nearest hospital.

At the hospital, a doctor put me on overnight watch. As I sat alone in a small white room, a nurse brought a glass of orange stuff and coaxed me to drink it. While my heart raced erratically, and my mind still fought the effects of the powerful hallucinogen I'd taken, I refused to drink the nurse's *potion*. My imagination soared as I pictured this drink to be a poisonous substance, she the evil plotting villain.

I sat in a corner of the room curled up in a tight ball and placed an invisible shield between me and the rest of the world—not talking, not daring to look at anyone. Perspiration seeped from my body's pores, and the odor I smelled seemed that of death. *Gotta get out of here before it's too late.* While my mind raced with thoughts of escape, I looked up and saw a girl sitting across the room. "Hi," she said in a soft, friendly tone. Her strawberry blonde hair glistened with health and vitality, unlike my own which was matted and tangled. Her name was Susan, she said, and she was a medical student working late on a report. Her voice soothed me, and I felt she could be trusted. Within minutes, this soft-spoken girl won my confidences then handed me the glass of orange drink. Reluctantly, I took it from her hand and consumed it. Soon, I fell asleep on a couch in the white room. When I woke up in the early morning hours Susan was gone, and the real world claimed me once again.

I hitchhiked back to our apartment and upon entering the kitchen saw Julie. "Where in the world have you been?" she asked.

"I thought something happened to you. Where did you go last night?" I queried.

"Catherine, I was at the party until early this morning; I looked everywhere and couldn't find you." I told her all that had happened and how I had seen her escorted away by the strange fellows and the guru. I soon realized I had hallucinated the whole nightmare. There had been no kidnapping nor had I turned into an old lady. It had all been an illusion, drawn up from the recesses of my drug-loaded mind.

After that night, I realized that unless something changed in my life, I would probably be dead before I turned twenty. As I heard the beckonings of Nature calling me out of the city once more, I decided to make another attempt to leave. This time I would make a cross-country trip. "I'm not coming back till I find the answers to life," I told my mother one day while visiting. It was as though I expected these answers to fall out of the sky in a neat little package, and all I needed to do was find the right spot to stand.

A gripping fear tried to surface at the prospect of being left alone on some highway in the middle of America. The images of my Canadian venture were still painfully vivid. Nevertheless, I spoke nothing of these thoughts. Instead, I pulled out my old army backpack and carefully stuffed it with all I would need. Along with an old Bible my grandmother had given me, went extra clothes, a blanket and an old sleeping bag. On side pouches I threw in soap, toothpaste, brushes, writing paper, a can opener and matches. There wasn't much to it. I wore no makeup, never curled my hair and certainly didn't have to worry about getting a run in my nylons. What remained in the apartment would go to the Salvation Army's bountiful heap of unwanted treasures.

I kissed my mother good-bye; she hugged me and held on tightly, hoping I would suddenly change my plans. I had a feeling this would be the last time I would live in California. We moved from the mountainous, tree-covered province of British Columbia a month before my eighth birthday. Now, eleven years later I was leaving California—this time something told me it would be for good.

I hitchhiked during the day and slept in a sleeping bag under the stars at night. Though apprehensive about hitchhiking alone, I would not allow myself to succumb to fear. My desperation to find truth and peace prevailed over any such feelings.

One day, shortly after I began my trip, a man who spoke little English picked me up. I no sooner sat my pack on the floor of his weather beaten van when he spurted out, "Hey, I geeve you hundrud dollas; you go to motel weeth me." He smiled broadly while patting the wallet in his pocket as if to surely entice me.

Oh great, I thought as I eyed this stranger. "Ah, no thanks. I'm not into that. Please, stop!" My heart pounded with anger and with fear. Hesitantly, he pulled off to the shoulder. I got out and took off walking at a fast, steady pace hearing only the scruffing sounds my boots made as they brushed against the gravel shoulder. Throughout that entire day not one decent human being stopped. As night fell, I made my way down the streets of El Paso, Texas, feeling lonely and surely looking bedraggled. My pack weighed heavy on my shoulders and back while my feet felt like they were going to fall off.

That night I slept in a Greyhound bus station, slouched in a corner of the woman's restroom with my backpack propped up against me. Tossing fitfully, I woke up often and pondered my situation. I could see no realistic way to get across the country, as long as I looked like a potential *good time* to every scoundrel that crossed my path. As I analyzed the problem, it dawned on me— I would have to avoid looking so available. *There's only one way to accomplish that*, I told myself.

In the morning, after a cup of bitter tasting coffee and a day-old donut, I headed for the nearest thrift store. For ten dollars I bought a floppy leather hat and a man's brown leather coat that came down to my knees. I buttoned up the coat, tied back my long hair and stuck on the floppy hat. The hat covered a good portion of my fair-skinned face. As I stared into a cracked mirror, I smiled at the image that could easily be mistaken for a guy, at least from a distance I hoped. I left the store satisfied and headed back to the highway

Up until then, catching rides had not been a problem. But as I sat on the freeway on-ramp under the warm, October, Texas sun, cigarette in one hand and harmonica in the other playing *Oh Susanna*, two hours passed and still no ride. People looked at the young hippie kid standing on the side of the road. Some waved, but didn't dare stop. Little kids giggled, staring wide-eyed while parents just shook their heads then looked the other way.

Finally, a car pulled over. A young longhaired fellow no older than myself offered me a ride. I tossed my pack in his car and jumped in.

"Hey man," he said. "I thought you were a guy."

Ah-ha, I smiled slightly. *It worked!* And it did. From then on, most of the people who picked me up thought I was some young hippie boy until after they stopped, and most of the time their intentions proved honorable. Those looking for a loose hippie chick to *have a good time with* didn't even blink an eye as they passed. It never occurred to me an unseen power greater than myself might be protecting me, watching my every move.

I traveled into the Northeastern states and ended up spending a couple days in Montreal, Quebec visiting a cousin I hadn't seen in years. She and her common-law husband were self-proclaimed communists. They preached a simple philosophy: there is no god, government is corrupt, and socialism is the only way for people to properly co-exist. As I left their quaint antique-filled house and hiked down the cobblestone streets of Montreal's Old Town, my ears were pierced with the lyrics of John, Paul, George and Ringo—*Imagine there's no heaven.* (And maybe no god?) Looking up at the blue sky, my heart ran fast towards the beat of a distant drum.

As my sore feet touched Alabama soil, a fellow hitchhiker I met said we should hop a train. What was routine stuff for a veteran traveler such as he though, was sheer terror for me. As we raced along side of the slow moving locomotive, I felt like this was true initiation into life on the road. Scared, but not admitting it, that my legs were going to be pulled under the train ripping my body in two, I ran like the dickens, grabbed onto the moving boxcar while my *friend* pulled me to safety. As I breathed a sigh of relief, I sat down looking out at the passing scenery.

We rode fifty miles, slowly careening past some of the poorest dwellings I had ever seen. The old, rusty tracks bore their intruding way through backyards, only a short distance from the wooden porches of houses that appeared to be barely more than cardboard shacks. Little black children played barefoot in the rock-filled dirt they called yards. We waved and smiled until they timidly waved back. I had been in the slums of some of America's largest cities but had not seen anything equal to this. Moms with their thick, coarse hair tied back in bandanas hung up their wash on thin, ragged lines. A look of silent longing pierced through their eyes of sorrow. They knew *they'd* never get out of this place. Maybe their dreams were for their children or maybe their children's children but certainly not for them.

Throughout the warm, breezy fall and into the cold, frosty winter, I covered thirty-nine states. In late December, I heard about a labor camp in Houston, Texas and decided to get a job for a week. More than once, people warned me Houston could be a dangerous city for a girl alone, and getting stuck on the streets when night fell could prove detrimental. So when I hit the city limits and dusk was quickly approaching, I made my way to the downtown bus depot. These had been safe havens several times already, and a cold wind rushing through the city left me with no desire to be outside.

That night, I curled up in a corner of the women's restroom, my boots and pack by my side. I pulled my thin blanket over my shoulders as I sat on the hard floor and leaned up against the wall. Soon I dozed off and dreamt of golden flowers dancing in the wind. In the middle of the night, a sharp, obtruding voice awakened me, "Wake up girl. Wake up!" Yawning while straightening up, my eyes focused on the face of a police officer. He glared with dark, sharp eyes. "You can't sleep here. You gotta leave."

"I can't do that," I pleaded. "It's the middle of the night." He looked at me for a moment as if in deep, serious thought, his bulky form blocking the doorway.

"I'll tell you what," he started, his voice changing to a gooey kind of sweetness. "I get off at six in the morning. You come to my place with me then, and I'll let you stay here the rest of the night."

Realizing this officer of the law was propositioning me, I denounced his vileness with cold defined words, "No way man. I'll leave!" I retorted hastily.

"Suit yourself," he said shrugging his shoulders as he turned to leave. "Be out of here in twenty minutes." Knowing this was a bad state of affairs, I now regretted having come into the big city at all. Slowly I rose to my feet, picked up my boots and pack, then headed into the semi-crowded lobby. Even at two in the morning this large metropolis depot was filled with people milling around.

As I sat down on one of the lobby chairs facing the front doors, I spotted the officer. He was conversing with three rough-looking characters who stood just inside the main entrance doors. Horrified, I watched all four men eyeing me intently as they huddled together in obvious conspiracy. It didn't take much to figure out they were up to no good. Without using much imagination, I knew as soon as I walked out of those doors trouble would be awaiting me!

When I was a little girl, my mother taught me a child's bedtime prayer. For many years, I repeated it each night before drifting off to sleep, almost superstitiously, afraid if I didn't say it something bad might happen to me. Then at eight years old, it seemed silly and unnecessary so I stopped. Prayer was as foreign to me as the ocean is to the desert. Yet now with my life in unmistakable danger I began, "God, if You're there, please help me. Please God, do something to help me."

As I tied the thick, yellow-striped laces of my brown boots, I paused from time to time hoping to stall for a few extra minutes. Visions of being jumped on and dragged to some dark, foreboding alley rushed through my head.

A voice interrupted my wide-eyed thoughts of rape and murder. "Hey man, what's happening?" Startled, I looked up into the gentle eyes of a young black kid. I hadn't seen him earlier in the depot; he was just suddenly standing over me. Feeling an urgency to tell him about the incident in the making, I explained how I suspected plans of foul play. "Yah, I know that cop," he said. "He's got a bad reputation," he whispered, intentionally lowering his voice. "Hold on a minute." And at that, this young kid, no older than I and about half the size of the officer, walked boldly over to the four men, said something briefly then returned to my side. He laid a hand on my shoulder then spoke softly, "Look, that cop is not going to bother you anymore. You can sleep here all night." He smiled as I looked up with relief and gratitude. "Oh and by the way, there's a little church on the corner. Why don't you come down in the morning and have some breakfast." Then he was gone. As quick as he had appeared he went away, and I never saw that boy again. I slept in the chair until dawn's early hours. The officer never came near me again.

I didn't stop at the church for breakfast and in fact forgot about the prayer. I didn't forget what happened though, knowing somehow my life had been spared.

A week later, I stood on the side of the highway in Arkansas, heading for a counter-culture farm community in Tennessee. The cold, north December winds whipped past my sun-tanned face as my long blonde hair blew loosely. The wind had already blown off my floppy, disguise hat, and I carried it at my side. A small blue pickup pulled over and was now honking. Embarrassed that I hadn't even seen it stop, I grabbed my pack, ran over and opened the door. "How far ya' going mister?"

"About twenty miles. You gettin' in or not?" he said with slight irritation.

"Yah, thanks for stopping." I hopped in and mentioned how the wind was picking up.

"Yep," he answered. I tried making small conversation as I often did. The man, who looked to be in his forties, kept his eyes straight ahead, avoiding eye contact. In fact, he had made no eye contact with me before I got in, a self-imposed rule I had made for survival on the road.

"Hey listen," he began. "I've got to get some air in a couple of my tires. I'm going to have to pull off for a few minutes." We had only gone a short distance when he turned off the interstate then headed for a small town running alongside the freeway.

"Would you mind letting me off here?" I asked. "You can pick me up on your way back through. I have this thing about never leaving the interstate," I lied. Something wasn't right, and a very bad feeling settled over me.

He continued to look straight ahead as he answered with smooth, slithering words. "Don't worry. You can trust me. This won't take long." We had already driven through the small Midwestern town and now began driving down a road which led further and further from the main road. It was clear to me now—he wasn't getting air for his tires. Suddenly, he turned onto a dirt road and picked up speed. Up ahead a mile or less lay a large, ominous section of dense forest. Only one thing was on my mind now—I had to get out of his truck. I yelled for him to stop, but he ignored my pleas.

Oh God, I prayed, once again calling out to an unknown deity. *Help me.* "Stop this truck," I yelled frantically. "And let me out!"

"Hey I told you, you can trust me; don't worry," he said with heightened intensity. His foot pressed further down on the gas pedal.

"Mister, you stop this truck NOW or I'm jumping out." At that, I opened the door and snatched my pack. Although he was clipping along at a good forty miles an hour, I knew my chances for survival were better this way than going into that forest with him. As I opened the door with every intention of jumping, he slammed on the brakes.

"Okay, okay, I'll take you back to the freeway." I leapt out of the pickup and took off running back to the main road. His plans foiled, whatever they might have been, the man sped off towards the forested area leaving a trail of dust and fumes behind. I never stopped running until I reached the so-called safety of the freeway. Tears stung my eyes as I wondered what in the world I was doing in the middle of the country, traveling alone, nearly having gotten myself raped or killed.

Frustrated and distressed, I held up my thumb and headed in the opposite direction of the farm in Tennessee. Christmas was coming in a couple weeks. I was going home.

Two

A Voice in the Barn

Jesus answered and said to him,
"Most assuredly, I say to you,
Unless one is born again,
He cannot see the kingdom of God."
Nicodemus said to Him,
"How can a man be born when he is old?
Can he enter a second time into his mother's womb
And be born?" Jesus answered,
"Most assuredly, I say to you,
Unless one is born of water and the Spirit,
He cannot enter the kingdom of God...
Do not marvel that I said to you,
'You must be born again.'"—John 3:3-7

Which way you goin'?" A young fellow-hiker approached me as I stood on a freeway on-ramp in Portland, Oregon. The cold Northwest drizzle had left me cold and shivering. Three months of poor eating and exposure to the elements left me thin, and I found it impossible to keep warm anymore. After relishing in my mother's love during Christmas, I hit the road again, still planning on going to the commune farm.

"I'm heading to Tennessee to a farm I want to check out," I answered the friendly longhaired boy. "How bout' you?"

"I'm headin' for Colorado. There's a huge gathering about to take place where the energy is going to be far-out. A lot of people have been waiting a long time for something like this. It's going to be a chance to get in touch with each other and the Earth and have all this outasight unity. Come along if you like."

"Yah, that sounds far-out," I answered. To say the least, it sounded perfect. *This has to be it,* I thought to myself. *This must be where the answer is. Finally, the chance I've been looking for. To think, all these people wanting to get in touch with the Earth ... and God? —The very thing I've been trying to do.* Standing at that freeway crossroad, looking one way then the other, I glanced at this young fellow, who by now had plopped down to feed his dog some granola.

Then as I stood there, a gentle, unfamiliar voice not my own, spoke to my heart, saying in absolute clearness, "Don't go to Colorado; the answer isn't there." Shaking off this peculiar nudging, I knew this was the moment of reckoning, the moment I had been waiting for, the moment I had been anticipating for so long. My golden opportunity stood smack in front of me, calling, beckoning.

And then without even knowing why, I declined the offer to go. The boy shrugged his shoulders, handed me a bit of granola and waved me a small good-bye. We went our separate ways, he off to a Colorado Rocky Mountain high, I going south, totally unaware that my seemingly undirected life was being governed by some unknown power.

With my stomach growling from hunger, I reached the southbound ramp and dropped my pack to the ground. I pulled the collar of my coat tight around my neck in a futile attempt to stay warm. Unbeknownst to me, the *very* next ride would change my life forever.

As I stood waiting for a car to stop, another kid, this one only about fifteen years old, came walking up the ramp. "Mind if I join you?" he inquired.

"No, I guess not. Where ya' heading?" I questioned.

"Los Angeles. That's where I'm from. I ran away about a month ago, but I'm goin' back to work things out with my mom."

"Yah, that's cool. Guess your mom's pretty worried about you."

"Maybe. Who knows?"

"Man is it ever crowded around here," I mentioned to my new young friend, Lewis. Ahead of us, standing further up on the freeway, we saw a couple other hitchhikers.

"Sure you don't mind me standing here with you? It could slow ya' down."

"Nah, that's okay." I said, patting him on the back. He didn't even have a pack with him. *He must have up and left fast. Poor kid,* I thought. Just then, we saw an old, blue pickup pull over several yards in front of us then coast slowly along the gravel embankment. Thinking they were pulling over for *us,* we ran towards them but stopped when it looked like they hadn't seen us after all but were stopping for the other hitchhikers. We watched as the two guys climbed in the back of the truck. And then, the driver of the pickup spotted us and waved us on. Lewis picked up my pack, and off we ran. Out of breath upon reaching the truck, we hopped in the back then dropped down on scattered bits of straw as the truck pulled out into fast moving traffic. Temperatures barely reached twenty degrees that morning, and with the wind whipping at our faces, it made for one blustery, winter ride.

Twenty miles out of Portland, the driver pulled into a rest area and offered a seat in the front for one of us. Well, since I was the only girl (though they'd taken me for a guy at first), the guys unanimously decided I should get the cab. I gave my blanket to Lewis then climbed into the warm cab.

As we rambled down the freeway, jaunting along at forty-five miles an hour, the two guys I now sat in between introduced themselves. The driver, Jered, was nineteen years old, the same as me. He had shoulder-length, brown hair and a cute Gerber kind of face. Tom, the other guy, was also nineteen. His long, straight blonde hair hung loosely around big brown eyes and tanned skin. Tom said little, leaving most of the talking to Jered and I, but his down to earth smile and kind eyes warmed my heart. The two of them lived in a little town called Peoria, where they shared a small trailer. Both fellows worked in a mill for a local farmer for $1.10 an hour. On the side, Tom raised sheep and a couple dozen chickens with the hopes of having his own farm someday. He was from Kansas—a place where I was sure farmers are as common as the corn.

After we dropped the other two guys off at their destination, Jered invited Lewis and I to stay at their place for a couple days through New Years. We took them up on their offer, and a couple days turned into six. During that week, Tom and I spent hours talking—it felt like we were kindred spirits.

"He's beautiful," I wrote of Tom in my journal, "a beautiful, sensitive person. Our ideas are so identical. We talk about farming, specifically about the plans for his farm. We talk about raising families, and although we never mention doing this together, it is as though we are asking one another if it sounds right; and it does, it surely does!"

Before I left, Tom and Jered told me to come back anytime, and I could tell they really meant it. One month later, they were utterly delighted to see me at their doorsteps one chilly afternoon. "How long you staying?" they asked with big smiling faces.

"Well, if I can earn my keep around here, guess I'll stay awhile." And that was how we became a family.

During the day while Tom and Jered worked at the mill, I took care of the chickens (and the dogs and cats) plus tended to any baby lambs.

I fell crazy in love with the animals. The guys raised the chickens for food, but I saw no way I was going to be able to eat them. To me, they were pets. However, Jered sternly warned me not to get attached, that they *would* end up on the dinner table before too long. Nevertheless, after some hard-hearted negotiations (I promised to bake chocolate chip cookies every day for a week), they agreed to let me keep one of the male chickens, to whom I gave the royal name of Henry. Henry stayed in a special place of his own, away from the other chickens. This way I could be sure he wouldn't end up on our dinner plates some Sunday afternoon.

One day, much to Henry's benefit and my sheer relief, he laid a small brown egg, and Henry became Henrietta, assuring her of a longer, more productive life.

As the cold rains of February whisked through our lives, March snuck in, bringing the very first soundless signs of spring. It still felt like winter, almost looked like the dead of winter, and only the keenest eye could spot the nearly invisible hints that new life was about to burst forth. Tiny cherry buds peeking through the branches, the bare tips of the crocuses timidly pushing through the still cold earth and temperatures just a few degrees higher than they had been, spoke of winter's end.

One day, the man who ran the general store told me about an old woman in a nearby town who needed a hand on her dairy farm. Edith Stewart lived two miles outside of Shedd, Oregon, a town about as big as its name suggests and only a few miles from Peoria. I decided to check it out.

As I approached the forty-two acre farm a few days later, I spotted a rustic long-in-need-of-repair barn and a green antiquated house, which looked like something out of Charles Dickens' *Great Expectations*. The house was seventy-three years old, Edith would later tell me, and had been built by her father the year she was born. The farm sat on the edge of the picturesque Calapooia Creek and was lined with patriarchal oak, maple and evergreen trees.

Sitting in Edith's dark, deteriorating living room beneath a multitude of cobwebs and dust that first day we met, I wondered what Dickens Pip would say at a moment like this. As Edith sat in an old stuffed chair in the corner of the living room, she leaned forward

A house much like the one on Edith's farm.

on her cane. Her dark, fierce eyes pierced me as she meticulously, with every detail included, recalled story after story of her father's courageous journey by wagon train from Ohio to Oregon, her husband's sudden death many years ago, and her blind aunt's tremendous ability to manage the farm almost single-handedly. Edith had been married once, and enjoyed only eight years with her husband before he was killed in a freak train accident. The one child they had was stillborn at fourteen pounds. Her blind aunt was the only one left to share in farm responsibilities. But now she too was gone, passing away with all the others, leaving Edith with a lifetime of memories and no one to share them with. Although most of them had happened decades ago, to her it seemed only yesterday.

Whatever I said about myself those first few minutes was really only heard by myself. Edith, more intent on studying me from top to bottom, carefully dissected, thoroughly analyzed everything she beheld: tall, thin, with long, straight, blonde hair and bright, blue eyes accented by blue overalls and rugged work boots. I doubted I was making a really great impression on this straight-laced, pioneer lady. I wanted so much to impress her too, hoping to get this job. I wasn't sure though how to tell her that I lived with two young guys *and* folks around town called us hippies.

However, Edith never asked about those things, and as I later learned, she didn't ask because she already knew. Before I'd even arrived, indeed minutes after we'd hung up from talking the day before, she made phone calls to all the right people, finding out everything anyone knew about Tom, Jered and myself.

"I can't pay you much cash, but you can have any spot in the barn to sleep, and I'll cook you two meals a day. How soon can you start?" I had just been offered room and board for exactly what, I wasn't sure.

With eager anticipation, I took the job. I could finally be on a farm and still be close to my new pals, Tom and Jered. My primary responsibilities included milking six cows twice a day, making sure all thirty cows and steers had hay available to them at all times, mending broken fences, planting a garden and about anything else that came to Edith's fast-thinking mind, either in the barn or in the field. I was going cold turkey into farm life.

The following day I gathered my things at the trailer, then moved over to Edith's barn. Picking a large, cleared out corner near stacks of sweet smelling hay, my new sleeping quarters lay only a few yards from the cows nightly eating area. An old, yellow sofa that looked like it had been stored in the barn for a hundred years became my bed; my bathing spot was now the Calapooia Creek. I felt a little like the pioneers Edith had spoken of.

One day, an old vanwagon pulled into the driveway. As Edith's two Australian shepherds barked madly and ran in circles, out jumped a shaggy-haired, bearded man whistling a bouncy tune while he made his way to the house. A few minutes later he and Edith came sauntering out to the back, Edith talking this chaps ears off as only she could do. "John, you've just got to see these hog heads," Edith boasted of her butcher friend's recent gift to us, which I was reluctantly cutting up for sausage.

"Well praise the Lord," he said with a hearty laugh. "God never ceases to amaze me the way He provides." I peeked around the corner, said hello then glanced down at a book he held in his burly hand. The book was a well-worn black Bible.

This is one happy guy, I thought, never having seen anyone quite so radiant before. And I'd certainly never seen anyone so earthy looking carrying a Bible. When I thought of Bibles, I thought of big expensive churches, sweet perfumed old ladies and organized pompous religion that thought little of the poor, mostly of money and definitely not God. I had decided a long time ago that if there *was* a God, He positively wouldn't be found in some richly adorned church building with people who wore suits, ties and stuffed shirts.

As I took another peek at this jovial man, his very presence blew away my idea of a religious person. His eyes twinkled as he stood talking, overflowing with obvious love and concern for Edith. After Edith returned to the house, John approached me and asked,

"Have you ever read the Bible?"

"I've got one, but I've never read it." I thought he was rather audacious to be asking such a personal question.

"Well," he said. "Why don't you try reading it? The Bible says if we really want to know truth we can ask God to show Himself to us, and He promises to do it." What made this stranger talk of truth, for I had certainly not inquired, was beyond me. Nevertheless, these things he told me, I had never heard such things before. Yet it made sense that if there *was* a God and if we really wanted to know Him, He would be kind enough to communicate with us somehow. So I thought,

I will ask God to make Himself known to me, and if there's no answer, then maybe there isn't a God after all. In the middle of this conversation with John, I promised to at least make an attempt to read the Bible.

Over the course of the following several weeks, in between milking cows and preserving food, I read through the first four chapters of the New Testament in my old Bible. As I read about this Jesus guy, I was very impressed with some of the things He did and said. He spent a lot of time defending the poor, actually coming down hard on the religious leaders of the day. He hated hypocrisy and loved being outside in Nature. It was obvious He esteemed women as highly as men and treated them with equal respect. The man wasn't afraid to speak his mind regardless of what people thought, nor was he too happy with the way the world system was operating. Moreover, he was a really radical guy with a lot of very strong feelings about matters of life and love.

I was reminded of other radical people I had heard about over the years. At one time, I had heard about a revolutionary group called the Weathermen. This group was known for its frequent bombings of wealthy establishments, denouncing anything that had to do with government and capitalism.

Now here was this man named Jesus who lived a radical life. He didn't go around bombing places, but he blew apart men's ideas of righteous living. Jesus denounced the arrogant

yet placed the humble in an honored position, and I could see He cared about man's suffering. The thought of Jesus as an extreme revolutionary never occurred to me before, but then I had never read first hand what the Bible had to say about him. The more I read, the more I came to see him as the most radical guy I'd ever heard about. There was just one problem, kind of a big one—he was dead. I mean the Bible said he rose from the grave, but that was a little hard to believe. Nevertheless, his teachings were cool and right-on, and that alone was enough to hold my interest.

John became a spiritual leader to me as well as to other friends I had made and would often expound on his interpretations of the Bible. I was amazed to hear how uniquely dissimilar his views were from what mainstream religion was. He believed living together for a man and woman was okay if a couple *felt* they were married in God's eyes. He believed marijuana was an herb of the Earth—an actual gift from God. He also spoke strongly against any kind of organized religion, that it was not genuine and at best could only fill churches with pews of hypocrisy. Although I later came to disagree with many of John's teachings, something was drawing me to the Bible like a bee to a honey-filled tree.

Eventually Jered decided to move back to his home state, Montana, and Tom moved over to Edith's with me. At Edith's suggestion, Tom built a small cabin on her property which became home for the two of us. Years later, I discovered the town's people appropriately nicknamed that cabin the *hippie shack*.

As summer came to a close and we prepared for hauling hay, I was still undecided over the matter, "Is there a God?" Nevertheless, I continued reading the Bible, determined to at least finish the New Testament. The week we started the hay hauling began as any other week. A lack of answers and nearly ten years of searching had left me feeling empty and exasperated. No matter how hard I tried, I could not come up with any concrete explanations. One minute I thought there must be a God, the next minute—nothing.

We set out that first morning just as the sun broke over the horizon, spilling reds and oranges into the pale blue sky. Our friend Rob, who came along to help, suggested we read the Bible on our way to the fields each day and during our lunch breaks. That morning, as Rob began reading, something peculiar happened—every word he read seemed to be alive, jumping out of the page, aiming straight at me. I wasn't sure if the others were feeling this too, but I kept saying, "Wow! That's far-out!"

"Yah, it really is," Rob added. It was like we were all being affected the same way, but I couldn't figure out how that was possible. In all the reading I had been doing, I had not *felt* anything. I had not felt that someone was actually talking to me, yet now, it was like this book was alive and was trying to communicate with me.

Throughout the six hay-hauling days, we gobbled up every word we read. Every time we opened the Bible, the words seemed living, piercing my very soul. It was no longer just an ordinary book but rather one abounding with life. Yes, it seemed to be breathing—the words, the letters, the pages themselves. And yet, who was this? Whose voice was this I could hear? Was this God? I realized something very strange was going on, something I couldn't even give a name to.

One evening out in the hay field, as we prepared to hook up the loaded trailer from the tractor to the pickup, one of the tires on the trailer went completely flat. Exasperated, I let out a slow, weary sigh, as Tom and Rob jacked up the trailer and removed the flat. Then Tom took off to town to repair it. Rob and I clambered up to the top of the load of hay, plopped down then leaned back against a bale, resting our sore backs and soaking in the soon disappearing sun. We read the final words in the second book of Corinthians: "Finally, brethren, farewell. Be perfect, be of good comfort, be of one mind, live in peace; and the God of love and peace shall be with you." *What a beautiful way to end a letter,* I thought.

We closed the Bible, looked up towards the setting sun and in astonishment, our mouths dropped open. In the horizon was the most incredible sight. The sun was just about to set behind the coastal hills and was partly covered with large, white, puffy and rose colored clouds. The cloud formation on the left side of the sun was identical to the formation on the other side of the sun. It was as though someone had painted a picture and using the most brilliant colors available, decided the picture would be absolutely symmetrical. There was not even the least bit of discrepancy from one side to the other. What we were seeing was virtually impossible, that clouds jetting hundreds of feet into the air could have such perfection and be identical to another cloud right opposite to it. I knew what we were seeing was humanly preposterous, unless … Rob broke the silence. Slowly he glanced over at me then turned his eyes back towards the sky.

"Do you know what this means?" he whispered, almost afraid to say anything at all. And at that moment, as the words spilled out of his mouth, I knew exactly what it meant. At that very same moment we both knew. There *was* a Creator, a God, a Maker of us all, and He had just taken the time to paint us the most beautiful masterpiece I could ever have imagined! No way was this an accident of Nature, no way an unintentional event. Indeed there was no way it had been created by man. It was God. It was as if a light was turned on after my whole life of being in darkness. The benefactor who was responsible for giving me life in the first place was suddenly there revealing Himself to me while I sat on a pile of hay. The moment carried too much sacredness to talk and so we sat watching, knowing, each knowing what the other was thinking and feeling—words were not necessary. Awestruck, I trembled and believed.

By the time Tom returned, the sun had long since gone behind the hills. The sky, now a dusky gray-blue, left no evidence of what had occurred only minutes before. We fixed the tire and drove back to the farm. As I fumbled, looking for the right words to describe to Tom the event that had taken place, he looked blankly at me, smiled and said, "That's nice." This moment was too special to be destroyed with plain, everyday words, so I quietly relished in the absolute certainty that God existed.

When we arrived at the farm, the fellows went straight to the house to report to Edith. I headed for the barn to let in the bellowing cows. It was late, and they were irritable, but as each found her own stall and dug into their molasses covered oats, the barn quieted down, and I began milking. The only noises were the quiet chewing of the girls along with the swoosh-swooshing sound of the milk machine. I sat on my little wooden stool next to the machine, stroking the side of a big red heifer, my back to the entrance of the room.

My mind wandered back to the day's occurrences and the stunning sunset that proved to me there was a Supreme Being. Yet I felt frustrated, not knowing who He was or how to approach Him, or if I even could. "Okay God," I quietly spoke. "If You *are* there, if You really do exist, then who are You?" As these thoughts poured through my head, I suddenly realized someone else was in the room. It was that kind of feeling of knowing someone is watching but not being able to see him. *Maybe one of the guys is in here*, I thought to myself. Slowly, I turned to face the doorway, sure someone would be standing there. At the very instant that I stared at the empty threshold, shivers went up and down my spine as a voice spoke. It was not an audible one but a voice so clear and defined it could well have been.

"It's me," the voice said. "Jesus." That was it, just those three words, but I knew it was real. And at that moment I knew the Jesus I had been reading about was not dead after all; He *was* alive! What the Bible said was true, and at that moment He stood in the room with me. I heard no other words that night, but a peaceful tranquility filled my heart. I was no longer aware of the sounds in the barn—the machine swooshing, the cows chewing. I only felt warmth throughout; I knew right then my search was over. All the years of looking for God since I was ten years old, not always even realizing it was God I was looking for, had culminated in this one glorious juncture of time. I had come close to believing the Earth itself was the answer, had thought for sure psychedelic drugs would illuminate my eyes, and thought for awhile it was in people themselves that truth could be found. But none of these things satisfied, none of them proved to me they were the way to life. I had been searching for a complicated answer and here it turned out to be the simplest one of all, a God who loved us, died for us and became alive again to live inside us. "Why did it take so long to see," I wondered aloud. "I am almost twenty and I never saw it before."

I finished up the milking, put the girls back out to pasture then started running up to the house anxious to share my news with the guys. Halfway up the path I stopped dead in my tracks. *What am I going to tell them? "Hey guys, guess what? I just met God!" They'll think I'm nuts. How do you tell someone you just met God? Would they even believe me? What, that Jesus Himself came to visit me in the barn while I was milking the cows?* I didn't understand phrases like *born again* or *giving your life to Christ*. All I really knew was God had revealed Himself to me, and His name was Jesus Christ.

I decided not to say anything right then. I would continue to read the Bible and find out all I could about my new friend. Yes, I felt that close to God to call Him my friend.

As the red and golden leaves of autumn fell from the valley's trees, Tom and I continued attending John's Bible studies, growing marijuana in the fertile soil by the river at Edith's (unbeknownst to her) and living together as though married. I fell in love with the Bible, reading page after page, getting to know this Jesus who was becoming my very best friend. Tom always went along with things, but he rarely said much, and at times, I sensed he thought I was rather fanatical to be taking this whole thing so seriously.

Summer ended and with its end came another change—I discovered I was two months pregnant. No sooner than Tom found out about the baby though, did he leave abruptly and return to Kansas for a visit with his family. He called me once a week, talking about coming back to get me soon and moving us to Kansas. I was against the idea completely, but John insisted it was my duty to follow my *husband* no matter what. Many of the teachings on pure, righteous living seemed to be excluded from his Bible studies but not the one of wives submitting to their husbands. It would be years before I was to learn the real meaning of a godly relationship between a husband and a wife and that God never intended for a woman to be without her own opinions and feelings. So without argument, without question, I left with Tom in November and moved to the Midwest. I said very little about it, but my heart was broken. I had come to love Oregon, the farm and our many new friends.

As we drove across the miles and miles of prairie land, heading for Tom's hometown, I loved the simple beauty of this Midwestern state. But when we arrived in the city and I met Tom's parents I wondered if we had made a mistake. His mom and dad were commanding, powerful folks, and it was obvious to me Tom was afraid of them, especially of his father. But they seemed eager to help us get settled ... and married.

Without further ado, Tom's mother decided we would be married down at city hall just as soon as possible. It all happened so fast. We had no ring; I had no pretty dress to wear, and Tom was so drunk on the day of the ceremony, he grabbed his brother's hand instead of mine when it came time to say the wedding pledge. Ralph, Tom's father, had already seen to it that Tom cut his hair, and his mother tossed out half of my clothes days after I arrived. For the quick, city hall ceremony she dressed me in a polyester, tailored man's shirt, saying anything else made me look too pregnant. Quietly, I tucked away the pretty flowered blouse I had hoped to wear. It seemed as if our lives were no longer our own while staying with them.

Fortunately, Tom found a job with a farmer, and we found a century old farmhouse to rent for $85 a month. This large, two-story house came with a barn, a chicken coop and a few acres.

We also managed to find a secluded spot for a marijuana patch. By spring, our *special* garden held over two hundred plants, enough to go to jail for, especially in Kansas. Nevertheless, we continued believing pot was a *gift* from God, and it was the conservative law that erred, not us.

Tom bought an old '51 Dodge pickup. I replaced my boots and overalls with new ones, and we bought chickens, a couple sheep and a few hogs. With the exception of not having our Oregon friends with us, we picked up where we left off, enjoying the pleasantries of a simple farm life. While Tom diligently scurried off to work each day, I tended to our big, white farmhouse,

Our rented farm house - It still stands today.

the animals and in the spring, a garden. Daily I read the Bible, and daily I smoked marijuana which I *knew* was giving me better insight. Soon I was full term with child.

Sarah Elizabeth was born in April. I hadn't the vaguest idea of what it was going to be like, but the moment I saw her I knew this was one of God's most magnificent miracles. I had never in my life been so overwhelmed with so much love for another human being. I was sure I loved her more than my very own self and could not get over the fact this baby had been created inside my body. I had entered the world of motherhood, the greatest job I would ever be privileged to carry out. In it would be my highest earthly joy and through it my most intense sorrow.

As a mother I wanted to do everything right—so afraid of doing anything that might hurt her. I really hadn't given sin much thought, at least not sin in my own life. In my foolish estimation, there was only one real sin of mine, and that was smoking cigarettes. I had tried quitting but was never able to manage it. Now with Sarah watching my every move I desperately wanted to be a good example.

Soon though, smoking cigarettes was no longer the only issue nagging at me. I had been tuning in regularly to a radio program that came on once a week over a local rock station. The show broadcasted clearly over radio waves from a farm community in New York called Love Inn. This large hippie-turned-Christian farm reached out across America declaring a message of God's love. I saw only one problem with these radical people—they had a very strong anti-drug message, insisting marijuana was used not by God but rather by God's enemy, the devil. Bothered by their ideas, I wrote to them, hoping to set them straight. They replied with a two-fold answer: first marijuana was illegal which ought to be proof enough God did not sanction its use and secondly they said, "There are many herbs and plants on the Earth but not all of them are intended for normal consumption, some even being poisonous." Still not convinced, I tucked these concepts within my heart.

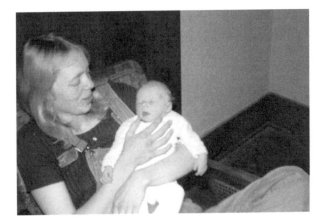

Then one afternoon in early fall while the baby slept peacefully in her crib, I sat on the couch, lit up a joint and opened my Bible. "Oh Lord," I prayed, as I turned to the book of Philippians, "please show me the truth about pot. I just don't know what to think anymore." No sooner were the words out of my mouth when I looked out the front window facing the road and much to my horror, saw a county sheriff car pulling into our driveway. Because we lived so far away from the city, a police car was a very rare sight. Jumping to my feet I raced to the back sunroom where nearly one hundred marijuana plants hung ominously overhead, drying. Panic embraced me at the realization of knowing there would be no way I could get them all down before the officer made it to the house, and there were still more plants growing outside.

Dear God, I prayed, *they will take away my baby girl and put us in jail.* Pushing my face firmly against the screen to get another look into the yard, I saw the car backing out and leaving. Not daring to move until the coast was clear, my heart beat fast and uneven as I watched until the car was no longer in sight.

Then one evening, as was our customary practice at the end of a day, Tom lit up a joint then handed it to me. I hesitated at first but then succumbed. After taking a drag, a strange, alarming sensation came over me. For some reason the drug was affecting me much too strongly. Feeling more like I was on a bad LSD trip rather than a high from a drag of homegrown marijuana, I thought about stories I'd heard of people who would have awful and frightening flashbacks. "Oh Lord," I prayed at that very moment. "If You will take this feeling from me, take away this high, I will never touch pot or any drug as long as I live." Instantly, as quick as the feeling had overcome me, I was back to normal with no high at all. The effects, whatever they were, disappeared. I stood up from the couch filled with a sense of awe and gratitude for this miracle.

Five years of pot smoking and psychedelic drug use ended that night. Whereas my whole drug era began with one single joint handed to me by a classmate, it all came to an immediate halt with one. God opened my blinded eyes, removing the deception that had often come close to destroying me. Drugs had clung to me like a leech in festering waters, often giving me a false sense of security and happiness, all the while sucking the very essence of life from me. The Lord healed me completely that day. In the nearly thirty years since then, I've never smoked pot or taken any other illegal drug nor ever suffered a flashback of any kind.

With drugs no longer a part of my life, my thinking processes cleared up right away. I began evaluating myself in a more honest way, seeing several other things that needed changing. Tom and I had not been getting along too well, and now that drugs were no longer a common factor we grew increasingly distant. We had no idea how to communicate with each other. I would cry and become emotional while Tom would simply close up even more, saying nothing. I desperately wanted him to talk to me, but he just wouldn't do it. I felt lonely and angry, thinking he didn't care enough to try. No doubt, he was feeling miserable too.

One afternoon when winter's cold had clearly made its showing on the Kansas farmlands, we were driving home from visiting some friends. I did not enjoy these visits anymore because it meant sitting for hours watching everyone get high, breathing in the now wrenching odor of marijuana. Often this caused a lot of tension between Tom and I. As we traveled home, driving along a back country road, I began telling Tom how insensitive he was. Saying nothing at all, he kept his eyes straight ahead while driving. In a dire attempt to get his attention, to get him to respond, I suddenly grabbed the keys out of the ignition and threw them out the window into a field covered with a foot of snow. Tom cursed while hopping out of the stopped truck. We spent an hour looking before we found them. I was broken hearted, angry with Tom, and angry with myself. We drove home in silence.

On that cold, November night, as Tom sat in the living room watching television and once more getting high, I sat in anguished solitude in our darkened, unlit bedroom silently weeping. I fell to my knees in humble exasperation crying out to God. Misery, self-pity, self-hate all filled my heart. No matter how hard I tried, being good, doing what was right just couldn't be attained. My *self* was in the way of getting close to God. For the first time in my entire life, I saw a perfectly accurate picture of myself—a sinner, lost and miserable and unable to do what was right by my own strength. I felt like a hopeless case.

As I remained on my knees for what seemed like hours, I prayed to my heavenly Father. "God, there's not much good in me, but if You want me, if You can change me, then I give You my life to do with as You want." It was a simple prayer. There was no one to lead me in a *sinner's repentance prayer*, but there in a big, old farmhouse in the middle of Kansas, all alone in that small dark room, God met me just as I was. Finally, when there were no more tears to shed, a tranquil sleep came. The gospel of Christ's death for our sins became a reality to me, as it never had before.

Early the next morning, as I lay alone in bed, I awoke feeling brand-new. A strong sense of God's love for me was in my heart. A small voice inside said, "Throw away your cigarettes." And without a moment's hesitation, I threw them away, just like that! I'd been trying to stop for over a year and suddenly was able to do it. I had no doubt in my mind that the strength was not my own.

A week later, Tom told me to go back to Oregon. He knew I hadn't been happy away from my friends, but the biggest problem had become the fact that I no longer smoked pot, and he did. It had been the dominant component we shared together, and now it was gone.

The following day, as we hugged good-bye at the bus depot, we renewed our love and commitment to each other, agreeing this would only be a visit. Unknown to either of us at the time, the Lord had planned this trip. For during the next three weeks I came to experience a deeper kind of fellowship and communion with the Lord in a little country church that our friend Rob was attending.

My heart became so full of joy and contentment, it was then I realized drugs had been a kind of pseudo-spirit, a fraud of the Holy Spirit. That was why so often while high I felt like truth was just barely out of my reach. Drugs imitated the Holy Spirit to a certain degree but then always fell short and would eventually lead right back to the original state—confusion and dark-

Peace and joy at last!

ness. The source of drugs and the high it gave was not from God as I had thought for so long but rather from the prince of this world, Satan himself.

For the first time in my life, I felt complete. I saw myself as a sinner, yet rejoiced in knowing that God had forgiven me. I saw God as the One who could take care of me and help me to become what He wanted me to be. It was like being a little baby who had just been born into a new world. Excitement captured me like a child going into a candy shop and being told, "Stay here as long as you like."

Before heading back for Kansas, a small group of believers gathered around me and prayed. Having never had a praying hand on me in my life, it was an unforgettable experience. One of the women standing in that circle quoted a scripture, saying she believed it was a word from God for my life. It was from Isaiah 55 and spoke beautifully of going out with joy, being led out with peace and how the mountains and the hills "shall break forth into singing before you, and all the trees of the field shall clap their hands. Instead of the thorn shall come up the cypress tree and instead of the briar shall come up the myrtle tree" (vs.12,13).

I had no idea what all of that was to mean in my life, in my future. I did not know that cigarettes and pot weren't the only things God wanted to take away. In fact, those would be trivial compared to the deeper work He planned on doing. I would come to find out that before the cypress and myrtle trees could rise within me, and in order for the briars to be destroyed, God would have to be allowed full reign in my life. Surrender along with unbounded trust in Him would be essential. The path would entail great suffering and sorrow, and yet these would be the very tools, the very fire God would use to destroy the thorns and briers. After that and only after that could the mountains and hills break forth into singing and the trees of the field clap their hands.

Three

He Loves Me, He Loves Me Not...

> Love speaks through your eyes,
> Caring, loving, trusting ... me;
> Love that never ends

"What happened to *you?*" Tom gasped in a whispered tone. He was at the bus depot waiting for us on our return from Oregon. Tom took Sarah from my arms, giving us both a warm hug.

"What do you mean?" I asked, puzzled.

"You look different, like you've got a big light on inside."

So it does show, I mused. It showed so much in fact, that later in the evening when I shared with Tom all that had happened, he fell on his knees, repented and gave his life to God. He said whatever it was I had he wanted it too.

Throughout that past year, I had suspected Tom really wasn't into all the Bible reading and talk about God the way I was. Yet this man so often remained quiet, never saying much of anything. He had always listened considerately as I read the scriptures aloud but showed no emotion, no real interest. Thus, I rejoiced when I witnessed my husband's genuine excitement for Jesus Christ.

The next six months seemed a near perfect portrait of a fairy tale marriage—we both enjoyed true happiness together, something only to be obtained when two people put Christ at the center of their union. Tom quit smoking pot and cigarettes, stopped drinking, and our fighting came to a halt as we spent much of our time reading the Bible together and enjoying our little girl.

On a radio talk show, we heard about missionaries, people who traveled to foreign countries to tell others about the Lord. Full of passion and zeal, we decided this is what we wanted to do with our lives—become missionaries. However, when we contacted a national missionary society, they advised us to get plugged into a local church and give ourselves some time to grow spiritually.

I was disappointed that we could not be missionaries right away; nevertheless, our lives radiated with joy and contentment. We loved our baby girl, we loved each other, and we relished in our newfound innocence as God answered our prayers quickly, at times even dramatically. Taking the advice of the missionary society, we joined a church.

Tom wanted to go to Bible school, and I still missed Oregon so we decided to move back so Tom could attend a school in Portland. As the fragrant lilac blossoms fell from their green bushes indicating summer's imminent arrival, we built a makeshift camper on the back of our '51 Dodge pickup. Filling it with clothes, mattresses and dishes, then with an *Oregon or Bust* sign nailed to the back, our dog and our baby by our side, we were off.

Tom and his parents cried when we left. Normally hard hearted, non-emotional folks, this was the only time I ever saw them break down. They considered it my doing that we were going back to Oregon and resented me for it, a resentment that would only grow over the years. They knew nothing about Tom's drug and alcohol problems. However, his younger brother informed them of my past, so from the beginning they felt I'd been a bad influence on him. My *religious* fanaticism carried no more acceptance with them than the drugs. They seemed far from realizing their son had a serious substance abuse problem. Tom was sniffing glue at the age of ten and claimed once that he'd shot up peanut butter just to get high. I had no idea his parents were the source and cause of all Tom's addictions and the reason Tom lived in a world tormented by fear, deceit and guilt.

At last though we made it out of town and away from what I had come to see as an oppressive grip on my husband's life. For the time being at least it became a thing of the past.

We no sooner settled into a turn-of-the-century apartment in southeast Portland when I discovered I was pregnant. Thrilled at the thought of another beautiful baby, we began our life in the metropolitan jungle. Tom started Bible school part time while working for various contractors as a carpenter's helper.

Eight months later, sweet little Rachael was born by emergency C-section. When Sarah was born, I never imagined loving anything as much as her, but when Rachael came, I found out that a mother's love isn't divided but rather it multiplies making room for another.

Being a wife and a mother fulfilled my ambitions and goals. I found it a joy cooking healthy food for my family and using creativity to make a fun and comfortable home. I could always find something more important to do than spend all day cleaning, but in between walks to the park and rides on the bus to the library with the girls, I made sure our home was clean and homey. It was a good life, and I never understood why women would *want* to leave their babies and go to work.

Tom's ongoing struggle to find steady work drained us. More than once he called his father to borrow money. Each time he squirmed as he listened to his dad's lengthy lectures on how Tom had messed up his life. Tom no longer attended Bible school, having only stayed about four months, and with school went his enthusiasm and interest in spiritual things. He started drinking and smoking again, then gradually withdrew from the kids and me.

One night, when Rachael was not quite two weeks old, as I painfully recovered from the C-section, Tom drove away shortly before dinner and did not return. Later in the evening close to midnight, as I rocked a colicky baby, a sudden rap at the front door startled me. Slowly I opened the door and looked up into the compassionate eyes of a concerned police officer. Tom had been picked up for drunk driving, and he would be spending the night in jail. With a grieving heart, I lay my now sleeping daughter in her bassinet and climbed into bed alone. Though Tom was never arrested again while we were together, drinking while driving became a habit he would practice for years to come.

Tom continued attending church with us. It seemed he really wanted to be close to God but just couldn't stick with it. Once, when an evangelist came to our church and prayed over several people, he laid hands on Tom and began praying for him. The man, who knew nothing about Tom, said he saw a picture of a cage with a bird flying around in it. The trembling bird was frantically trying to flee. There was something peculiar about this for the door to the cage was open, yet still the bird couldn't seem to escape. The evangelist said something in Tom's life resembled that bird. God had opened the door for him to be free, but some unknown factor kept him from flying out the door. How could I have known or have fathomed that a dark decaying secret had haunted his family long before Tom was ever born?

Frustrated with our marriage, I tried hard to be happy and content, but inside I felt terribly wounded, wanting a godly husband—someone I could look up to and depend on. Sometimes at night, while Tom slept, I wept, praying for us to be close but not knowing how to accomplish it.

Tom hadn't any successful relationships, not with men or women. He seemed more afraid than anything else of most people. He was terrified of his father. On the phone to Ralph, Tom often lied about the details of his life. If Tom had been given a dollar an hour raise (an impressive raise in the seventies), he would tell his father he received a two-dollar raise. His greatest nightmare, one far beyond normal limits, was his father's disapproval.

Soon I noticed Tom's deceptions extended to other people. As if he believed this world of lies he constantly created, he was no longer able to distinguish falsehood from reality. In our lovemaking, he was quick and unemotional. I felt more like an inanimate object with him than his wife. Whatever transpired in his mind was a complete mystery to me; I heard only silence. The silence grew stronger … and louder.

Occasionally the feeling of being lost in a race without end overwhelmed me, and I became almost hysterical in a futile attempt to get some kind of reaction from him. When this happened, my husband merely looked at me so much as to say, "You're nuts." Still, he never said a word. A lonely dejection ate a hole through my heart as I came to understand this was going to be my burden to carry.

One cool, breezy afternoon while the two girls took their naps, I fell to my knees in our small family room with the mid-day sun dropping golden rays down on my back and cried out to God. I prayed for Tom and for our family. Suddenly, a scripture popped into my head, and I felt the Lord urge me to read Proverbs 29:1. Reading the verse, I knew right away it was a picture of my husband, "He who is often rebuked and hardens his neck, will suddenly be destroyed and that without remedy." I felt the Lord telling me:

"If Tom does not repent, I will take his family away from him forever." At first it frightened me as I wondered if God was warning me that the children and I were going to die unless Tom changed. Yet how could I tell him? He wouldn't believe me but would only see this as a wife-nagging tactic.

No, I simply cannot tell him. I jotted down the date in my Bible, then rose to my feet with a sense of helplessness welling up within.

That evening when Tom arrived home from work, he made a beeline directly to the kitchen where I stood over the sink scrubbing carrots for dinner. "There's something I have to tell you," he said softly. "On the way home tonight, I was going to stop for a drink when I believe God told me that if I didn't change my ways and follow Him I was going to lose you guys." Stunned at this *coincidence,* I then spoke in detail of the afternoon's occurrence, show-

ing him the notation I'd written in my Bible.

So moved by this apparent sign from God, by the next day Tom seemed like a totally new person. He stopped smoking just like that, quit drinking and became the loving person he had once been. It was a glorious time. We laughed and did things together as a family. I forgot about the difficult past and dared not think of the future. The present brought laughter to my soul.

In February 1979, I gave natural birth to Matthew Josiah, who weighed a hefty nine pounds, six ounces. When our good friend, Leslie, saw him, she laughed and said, "Why, he looks just like a little man." Being a helpless baby was not Matthew's idea of a good time. He rolled over at only a few days old then lifted his head shortly after that as if to say,

"I'm strong and independent. I'll figure this all out." He proved such to be true when at the age of five he would do the bravest thing any child could do.

Tom did not believe in birth control though he never really gave me any reasons except that he didn't want me "taking nothing or putting anything in my body." I was glad for all my precious babies, but after having three in four years, I was in need of a break. Tossing out literature on diaphragms and birth control pills, Tom told me not to worry about it—that it would all work out.

Unfortunately, Tom's recommitment to Christ lasted a very short time, partly due to a group of people who had joined our church. This group brought with them the unbiblical word-faith doctrine that taught if you had enough faith in God you need never suffer or go without life's pleasures. If you were poor, unemployed or sick, it was because of a lack of faith.

The leader of this group approached Tom one day and told him we struggled financially because he did not

Sarah, Matthew and Rachel

have enough faith. Though our pastor eventually asked this group to leave our church, Tom could not get over the condemnation put on him. I watched in agony as he grew bitter and angry and slipped right back to where he had come out of, only this time his depression was deep and unreachable. Tom never hit the children or me. He was especially kind to the children. Nevertheless, his silent, obscure behavior tore away at my very life and was far more painful than a hard slap in the face.

My self-esteem plummeted as I fervently wished for a successful marriage, continually blaming myself for not having one. *It's my responsibility to make this work*, I told myself. Even as a child, I felt a sense of responsibility for everything and everyone around me. Once at the age of eleven, a small gray mouse had been unwarily caught in a mousetrap in our garage. Carefully I removed the bleeding, whimpering creature, begged for a small dose of sleeping medicine from my mother, then fed it to the dying victim, hoping to ease its last suffering moments. Minutes later, it died in the palm of my hand, and I cried. Now I struggled with the unyielding responsibility of my marriage.

With Rachel in Portland

The thought of leaving Tom crossed my mind more than once, but in my heart I knew God's blessing would not be there if I did. So I resolved to stick it out no matter what and pray that someday God would answer my prayers, giving me the godly husband I desired and the nurturing father the kids needed.

I wanted to behave and think as God desired. I was determined to adjust, to be satisfied with what God had given me. Somehow, through God's grace I would become the kind of wife Tom needed.

That is why in the spring of 1980 when Tom came to me one day and said he wanted to move us back to Kansas, I agreed. He insisted it would be good for the children to be near their grandparents and that his father had promised to help him find a better paying job. I didn't want to leave Oregon again. Yet, when I saw how Tom perked up so much from the idea, I thought it might be the very thing to bring him out of his depression, thus allowing us the chance to become close again.

Two months later, we headed for Kansas. Memories of the Midwest's massive blue sky and of the air radiating with cleanness were

1980—Rachel and Sarah

rekindled. Returning to the endless miles of farmland and anti-quated farmhouses filled me with optimism towards the future.

While we traveled from state to state in a large U-Haul truck, Tom spoke few words. I entertained the kids with coloring books and every song I knew as we passed the days peacefully. However, when Tom told me he had been smoking pot again, we got into a big argument. Knowing marijuana was back in the picture again frightened me. I tried to push the fear aside and hold onto my hope that this move would bring a positive change.

When we reached my in-law's home, they decided we would stay there a few weeks until Tom started working. In spite of my hopefulness, things went from bad to worse. *Surely*, I thought, *his folks are overjoyed at our return and will not harbor their earlier resentments towards me.* Yet from day one, there was a coldness I could not inter-pret as anything but resentment and dislike. Unusual things happened, things I tried to ignore but soon picked up as signs of hostility. It started out with such oddities as neglecting to set a place for me at the dinner table and later Tom's mother serving after-dinner coffee to a number of adults, bringing each person coffee in her best china then bringing me mine in a Styrofoam cup. I said nothing, but I hoped these oversights were just that. Soon though the family was excluding me from all conversations and any outings.

In the evenings, Tom and his father would go into the study and spend hours away from the rest of us. When I asked

Tom once what they talked about, he snapped at me with a peculiar coldness I'd not often seen in him. One evening when I passed by the study door, stooping to pick up a toy dropped earlier by a playing toddler, the study door flew open. There, glaring down at me, stood my father-in-law. He never said a word but gave me an icy look that sent shivers up my spine. *Whatever are they talking about*, I wondered, *that would make him so suspicious?* Later that night, Tom asked me what I had been doing eavesdropping.

One morning, I woke up feeling nauseous and exhausted. "Tom," I said, "I wonder if I'm coming down with something."

"You're probably pregnant," he said with a sarcastic sneer. Hearing the words, I feared them to be true. Tom told his parents, and from that day on, Ralph never spoke another word to me. If he walked into the room, he greeted each person but acted as if I wasn't even there. Hilda, Tom's mother would talk to me, but I knew she was upset. I wanted to tell them how I had asked Tom to let me use birth control, but he was dead set against it. I wanted to tell them that it was as much his doing as mine, but again I said nothing.

Tom wouldn't talk to me, let alone look at me, and when he did, he seemed angry and irritated. He spent countless hours away at his brother's place, his brother who was into drugs and heavy drinking. In the evenings when Tom was home, most of his time was spent in his father's study. What little connection I still had with my husband while we were back in Oregon now quickly disintegrated in Kansas.

One night, as we sat around the dinner table, Ralph finally made contact. He hadn't spoken directly to me in days. He was holding a flashlight in his hand when suddenly he shone it straight into my eyes. I laughed a little, thinking he was joking around, but when I asked him to stop he continued the game all the while piercing me with his cold eyes of steel. It wasn't a joke, no one was laughing. It was a tactic of intimidation, something Ralph was very proficient at.

Finally, after three weeks, we found a cottage-style house in a small town outside the city. We paid rent on it but could not move in, Tom said, until we bought a refrigerator. More anxious than ever to get into our own place, I felt more like an intruder than a houseguest at my in-laws home. On top of that, it seemed like I was losing my husband. So one afternoon when Tom returned from his brother's place, I managed to get him alone. As we stood facing each other, I asked him if we could move in right away. When he agreed to this, I hastily rushed to pack our things. Quickly, I folded blankets, washed sheets and tidied up the rooms. Within two hours, we were packed and ready to go.

Hilda had been to the circus with the kids and upon returning saw our bags sitting by the front door. Hastily she stormed out of the room, found Tom and wanted to know why we were moving out. I never found out what went on in that conversation, but Tom came to me a few minutes later very coldly stating, "You've upset my mother. We're not moving out; you'll just have to wait." My eyes filled with tears.

"Please Tom. I think things will be much better once we get into our own place again."

"We're going to wait," he said, raising his voice. I proceeded to fill him in on all that had been happening, explaining how his parents' resentment and rudeness were wearing me down. "You're making it all up," he snapped. "It's you that's got the problem; you're the whole problem around here. We're *not* moving out until I say so, and we won't go until it's fine with my folks."

With my eyes welling up with tears, I called to the girls, picked up the baby and a couple diapers then ran out the front door. We walked along unfamiliar streets until we came to a large, grassy park. As the children played on the swings, I called Tom from the park's pay phone. "Listen Tom," I began, trying to hold the tears back. "I can't spend another night in that house— maybe we should go back to Oregon; maybe coming here was all a mistake." I felt devastated over the way things were turning out.

About an hour later, Tom picked us up in his parents' car and said he would drive us to the new house. He made no eye contact as the late spring sun warmed the inside of the car. Then out of the blue he said, "I think we need a cooling off period, Catherine." I sat listening to this man who had become a total stranger to me.

"What do you mean?" I asked, looking intently at my husband.

"I'm not going to move out there with you," he answered curtly. I studied his face, looking for some sign that he really didn't mean this but instead saw only a stoic glaze in his eyes. In fact, he appeared to be in a trance-like state. The bizarre thought crossed my mind that maybe he was hypnotized, something his parents had practiced for years. Shaking such thoughts, I wondered why Tom had been acting so strangely, so distant and bitter since we'd arrived. He'd always been quiet, often depressed, but I rarely saw him hostile.

My soft crying turned to heavy sobs as I begged him not to go. However, he gave no indication of relenting. All the way to the house, I neither saw nor heard anything outside the confines of the car; as we drove through the city and out into the country, passing houses, pastures, people and cars, they were nothing more than a blur. Crying came easy as the tears, which had been bottled up for so long, were released. I could not bear the frightening thought of my husband leaving.

As we pulled into the gravel driveway of the small red and white house, Tom seemed to soften. Maybe seeing the brilliant colored flowers lining the white picket fence brought him to his senses or taking in the fragrance of the sweet smelling lilac bushes reminded him of why we were here—why we traveled half-way across the country. Maybe for a moment, as he gazed into the eyes of his two little girls and his baby son he remembered who we were, that this was his family, and till death do we stick together. To my relieved surprise, he agreed to take his parents' car back, get ours, then return. It was as if the invisible hold his father and mother had on him was temporarily broken. *Has it been their doing that kept him away from me these past three weeks? Why? How? How could a grown man be so easily drawn into the spell, yes, the spell of these people?* When Tom left, he promised to be back in a couple hours. He never returned.

Trying to assure myself that he would come home, that he just needed some time alone, I dropped into bed late that night. My eyes burned from crying. Exhausted, I hoped for a peaceful rest. Sleep did not come though. Frightening speculations raced through my mind. I was encumbered with anxiety. As more tears came, so did alarming thoughts, grabbing deeply at my heart. Every noise startled me while a late night wind blew against each window, trying to find its way inside but able only to leave an old house groaning and creaking in the dark.

Feelings of isolation hit like a hard slap, as if God had gotten in that car and left too. My thoughts drifted back to mistakes I had made, words I had said. *Maybe this is God's way of punishing me for everything I've done wrong. If only I'd been a better wife, perhaps he wouldn't have left. But oh how I have tried.* "Lord," I questioned, "have all my efforts, all my prayers been entirely in vain?" At last … sleep came.

Early in the morning, I woke to the now familiar nausea. That afternoon the local health clinic confirmed my suspicions. I was four weeks pregnant! Day after day passed. Every morning the children and I made the long walk up town to call Tom, and every morning his parents said the same thing, "He's not available." After three days, I told them we had practically no food and only a few dollars. The following day an envelope arrived in the mail bearing five dollars!

Is this some kind of sick joke they are playing? Me perhaps they despise, but the children—I don't understand. We ate spaghetti noodles with catsup for breakfast, then again for dinner. We joked about the noodles and sang songs every night before going to bed. Though inwardly I was being ripped in two, I was not going to let this destroy what was left of my family. Though I was suffering from this heartbreak, I was determined my children would not.

One day, I took the children to a nearby park, hoping to make life as normal for them as I could. At the park, they played on swings and danced on a carousel, laughing and running while

I rested on the grass. I was amazed by the quiet stillness in the air. Not a soul could be seen anywhere. Dark, shadowy clouds covered the blue sky. Then, just as suddenly as the stillness had set in, there came a strong breeze of warm air. It felt refreshing after the blistering, muggy day. *Ah, these small Midwestern towns*, I mused. *Why you'd think the whole town would be out on an evening as gorgeous as this.* A man's rough, hurried voice interrupted my fleeting thoughts.

"Hey lady! There's a tornado on the way; you'd better get home!" Waving me on, he rushed back into his house across the street, slamming the door behind him. For a brief moment, I froze.

What is a tornado? I frantically wondered. They were rarely mentioned on the West Coast. I knew only one thing about them—one had carried Dorothy and Toto over the rainbow to a land of munchkins and wizards. Quickly I jumped up, lifting Matthew off the ground. The lovely breeze had now turned into hefty blasts of cold wind.

Trees swayed rampantly back and forth. The swings, which the children had played on just moments before, were crashing and banging against one another. The wind was loud, making it difficult to hear each other. "Girls," I shouted, "we've got to run as fast as we can." The wind had picked up unbelievable momentum, and we were only able to move at a slow pace. Carrying the baby in one arm and holding Rachael's hand in the other while Sarah clung to my shirt, we labored towards home. Trash cans flew into the streets while a decrepit looking cat ran against the current, trying to find its way to some secure shelter.

Breathless and shivering, we arrived home and headed for the basement, which seemed to be the safest place. Although it was dingy and gloomy, it was a welcome alternative to the raging storm. Quietly we huddled together, wrapped in an old wool blanket, listening … waiting … hoping we would not be taken to a far off land of witches and magic. Finally, in spite of the children's fearful protests, I hurried upstairs and grabbed a radio. The tornado had touched down on the other side of town and was now miles away. Weary and drained but so very relieved, we climbed the stairs then fell exhausted into our beds.

With our telephone now connected, I felt certain Tom would call that night. *Surely, he's heard our little town has been hit by a tornado and will want to know how we are.* As the telephone remained quiet, disappointment and rejection wrapped their frightening tentacles around me. In the late hours of the night, I fell into a restless sleep.

Each day became an extension of the day before, none of them having any end nor any beginning. Life was a blurred vision of unreality. I wasn't even sure God was with us. I couldn't pray, couldn't hope. I was scared at night and terrified of the future. I called some local friends of Tom's. "No," they said, "We haven't seen Tom at all." When I told them I thought it was the doing of Ralph, they thought it could be true. They told me things I'd never heard before, stories of Ralph's mistreatment of Tom when he was little—degrading name-calling and locking Tom in the basement when he was very young. No, it didn't surprise them at all that Ralph was in on this.

In my despair after many sleepless nights, countless miserable days, I cried out to God, begging for His presence and His guidance. Within hours of that prayer, a gentle peace began settling over me. I had always heard that in times of great trauma God's grace becomes supernaturally evident. Somehow, I knew this unexpected peace was indeed His gracious touch. Though only seeing glimpses of His faithfulness at the time, it was enough to sustain me, and I realized God had not left us nor would He ever. Whereas human love has many limits and conditions, God's love never ends. No matter what might happen, I felt He would be there.

After several unsuccessful attempts to contact Tom, including a call to him from my own father, word came from my mother-in-law that Tom was not coming back. Ever! In the same breath, she asked to see the children—could she make a visit? A neighbor woman whom I had confided in warned me that if my in-laws came and took the children and kept them, it could take months in the courts to get them back.

My mind wandered back to a scene three years earlier. I was twenty-two and eight months pregnant with Rachael; Tom and I had once again grown distant from each other. As we stood looking at each other in our small city apartment in Portland, I told him I didn't think I could take much more of our problems. Suddenly, without warning, he snatched Sarah off the floor and ran out the door with her into the cold February weather. I stood in stunned silence as if watching a scene from a movie. *She doesn't even have her coat,* I realized in a frenzied state of shock.

I waited for hours, well into the night, but they never came back. By the following day, I was near total exhaustion. On day three, my parents insisted I fly down to California to wait there, as they were concerned for my health and the health of my unborn baby. With special permission from my doctor, I boarded a plane and flew to California. When a week passed, we finally heard from Tom. He had taken a bus back to Kansas and was not sure, he said, that he would be coming back. Near collapse from lack of sleep and worry, my father interceded, speaking with Ralph.

"I think it would be best if Tom brings Sarah back. We both know who will be paying the attorney fees if this thing goes to court." My father hit a nerve that was close to Ralph's heart—money. A week later, Tom returned with my baby daughter. For days after, she clung to me and would not leave my sight for a moment.

Now here I was in the middle of Kansas defenseless and surely not able to thwart single-handedly any plans my in-laws may have to take my children. The odd and cruel behavior they displayed and the total, sudden abandonment by my husband left me terrified the family was up to no good, and taking my children from me may be very well on their minds. *If only Tom had given me the least indication he still cared, if only he'd given me more than silence; but I don't know this man anymore. Maybe I never really did.*

Using money my father had wired me, we left Kansas on a greyhound bus and returned to Oregon. Too humiliated to face my friends and church in Portland, we found refuge in a rural setting with Donnie and Virginia, two of my old hippie-turned-Christian friends. For a month they enveloped us with their comfort, assuring us that God still cared. We then returned to Portland to wait there for Tom's return.

On January 21st, while millions of people across the country watched the final exciting minutes of the Super Bowl, Peter John was born. It was a perfect day for a boy who would grow up loving sports. Though Peter was born unbreathing from a knotted umbilical cord, doctors resuscitated him back to life, and he hasn't stopped moving since. I have yet to see his enthusiasm for life outdone by any other person.

As the months ticked by, life produced a hub of constant activity. Sarah attended a small Christian school in which an anonymous donor from church paid the tuition. Rachael and Matthew played in our picket-fenced yard with the neighborhood children who frequented our doorsteps. Our weekends were sprinkled with trips on the metro bus to parks, libraries and museums, all delightfully entertaining and fitting our very limited state-assisted budget.

We spent countless hours at home reading books. Curious George, Babar, the Elephant and Peter Rabbit lived inside our imaginations taking us around the world from Africa to Mr. McGregor's lettuce garden. Sunday mornings started by sleeping until I was tackled by four bouncing, giggling rascals then dressing in our very best (ironed to perfection) and piling into our brown '66 Plymouth Valiant to go to church. And of course, not a weekday afternoon passed when our used television set was not turned to *Little House on the Prairie*.

I discovered comradeship with two other single moms and likened single parenting to a war-torn country during tumultuous times. Leslie, whose sweetness and wisdom was like ointment to a wound, and Theresa, who had this uncanny ability to find humor in the most dire situations, became allies on the battlefield, supporting and understanding me as no one else could do. When we weren't crying on each other's shoulders, we were laughing at the whole hilarity of being abandoned and forgotten by ones who had promised to love us till death do us part.

One warm spring day, nearly a year after Tom had been gone, there was a knock at the door. My disappearing husband had reappeared. As he plopped himself down on our over-stuffed couch, I observed his slurred speech and silly mannerisms meaning only one thing for Tom—he was drunk.

"I want to move back in with my family," he stated abruptly.

"Tom, before you do that, I will have to have your word that you will never leave us again. I wouldn't be able to go through this again. It has torn my life in two. And before you move in, we must get some counseling."

"I am not going to get any counseling," he said emphatically. "You get it if you want but not me."

"Can you make a commitment to this family that you will never leave again, no matter how hard things get?"

"I can't make that kind of promise. If things get bad, I'm not staying. You're being unreasonable."

"In that case Tom, I don't think it's a good idea for you to move in … not now. I know I couldn't go through this again."

Realizing he wasn't going to be able to regain possession without at least some effort *and* some communication, Tom became furious. As the children stood by confused and frightened, they watched while their father grabbed my arm and yelled, "You're ruining these kids' lives. They need a father!" Pulling my arm away from his grip, I answered, "Tom, please leave. Don't ever come back here drunk again." He walked out the door and that night went on a small rampage ending in a fist fight with an old friend of his. He left town the next day.

In the years we'd been together, I had never seen Tom violent as he was that night. He was ruining his life and drowning in his own debris. I felt sorry for him but knew it was not up to me to change him. I had tried doing so before, and it didn't work. I placed him in the hands of the One who could change lives.

In the fall of my second year alone, when Peter was not yet a year old, I started attending a few classes at the community college, seeing this as an avenue to adequately support my kids. As I thrust myself into writing and math classes, I found college to be a wonderfully rewarding challenge. I had attempted college a few months after high school graduation but found it boring and irrelevant. Now however, I gobbled up the myriads of information. Though homework took up a lot of my time in the evenings, I was only away from home twelve hours a week.

Then one spring morning, when the air was filled with gentle winds and fragrances of jasmine trees and lilac bushes, the telephone rang. It was Tom. More than two years had past since he had left, and we were now divorced. "I'm moving back to Oregon; I want to see my kids," he boldly declared.

I didn't think Tom would ever show up to see them. He'd shown absolutely no interest in any of us for so long.

He had definitely lost interest in me—the children though were another matter. I was gravely concerned about Tom seeing the kids alone, not able to pinpoint my anxiety, but one thing for sure, Tom would not be a good influence on them.

In a dire attempt to halt overnight visits, I made an appointment with Legal Services, a legal agency for low-income families. "I'm afraid my husband is going to hurt my children," I told the attorney.

"What makes you think that?" she asked, looking skeptically over her wire rimmed glasses. I had wished at that moment, seeing her cold, apathetic attitude, I could have hired a regular attorney instead of this service for the poor.

"Well, he drinks a lot and smokes pot."

"Oh for goodness sake," she retorted, "lots of people do that!"

"I'm also worried he may try to molest them." It had become an underlying concern. Though I didn't think Tom would actually do such a thing, I felt he had the potential. Things he had told me before we were even married seemed like no big deal then. But now the youthful naivete I had possessed at nineteen was slowly disintegrating as I met women who had been sexually abused by their own fathers.

"Well now, that's a different story. Do you have proof he's done this?"

"No, he hasn't done anything *yet*, but I think he could. He told me once that he'd been involved in a homosexual relationship before he met me (I had always suspected it was with his old sheep farming partner, Jered), and he also grew up with a lot of pornography around."

"I'm sorry," she said, "these things are not proof he is going to molest your children. If something happens, you let us know." Later this curt answer would haunt me.

The eve before Tom's first visit, I called him. "I just want you to know, Tom, I've warned the kids about good touches and bad touches. Don't ever touch these kids in a wrong way." Click!

He hung up, but I felt satisfied.

At least I have warned him. I have covered the ground. There is no way he'll ever try anything now, I assured myself, *knowing I'm aware of such things.* That was the only time I ever said this to him. And although I would periodically remind the kids about good touches and bad touches, I never referred to my initial suspicions of their dad. I did not want to turn the kids against him by bad mouthing, which I was sure would only confuse them. As long as I maintained an open line of communication between my children and was the best mother one could be, praying for them, giving them a sound, moral home, as long as I did these things—they would be fine. No one could hurt them. After all, I wasn't anybody's fool.

Four

Little Eyes, You've Seen Too Much

Little eyes,
I think you've seen too much,
Of this sinful ol' world.
Can't help but wonder,
What you're thinking of.

Little child,
Let me take your hand,
And lead you to a place
Where God has total reign.
He'll dry your tears,
And soothe your heart.

Little one,
How I love you
And long to keep you,
In my bosom
But I know that someday —
I'll have to let you go.

Tears rolled down five-year-old Rachael's cheeks. Frantically she sucked her thumb. Wisps of soft, blonde hair matted against her wet face; I leaned down and picked her up. "Don't you want to go with daddy, honey?" I asked gently. With thumb still in mouth, her big brown eyes pleading with me, she shook her head. Oh how I wanted to keep her with me; how I wanted Tom to let her stay that weekend. It was his second overnight visit with the children. He became angry for what he said was my mishandling of the situation. Reluctantly, in order not to upset Rachael even more, I handed her over to Tom. When they left, I cried and begged God to watch over my babies.

That was the only time Rachael ever put up a fuss when going with her dad. It never occurred to me that he might have threatened her, may have scared her out of her mind. None of the kids ever protested in going with him. Though they never mentioned his name at home, never showed any interest, they never said a word about not going.

Every time they drove off, every time they walked out the door, they were on my mind until their return. I thought about them continually.

Just prior to Tom's first visit, the children and I moved from Portland to a much smaller community. I didn't want to raise them in a city where they would have to play near freeways and skyscrapers instead of evergreen trees and rivers. I enrolled in college again, my second year towards a journalism degree. Between endless homework assignments and perpetual housecleaning, my alone weekends passed quickly. The best moment of all came when the kids raced through the house, jumped into my arms with shouts of ecstatic glee, and for

Matthew
2 Months After Visits Began

two weeks until his next visit I wouldn't even let myself think about Tom. We immersed our lives with reading books, trips to the park, eating healthy food and watching *Little House on the Prairie*. We attended church services twice a week and loved to sing whenever we could. Though my heart ached for the situation we were in, I was determined to provide my children with a happy home.

When I had been alone for nearly three years, and the word dating was as foreign to me as atomic theory, I met a man at our church who started coming around to visit. Martin was a single deacon at church, and was a gentle man with a servant's heart. It didn't take much time before I was head over heels for him, and he seemed equally interested. *At last*, I thought, *I might have the godly man I have so longed for.*

Then one evening Martin informed me he thought we should stop seeing each other because he could never marry a woman with four kids, and he was afraid I might become too emotionally involved if we kept up the relationship. I broke into tears, feeling like a schoolgirl who had just lost her first boyfriend. Martin tried to console me, but my heart was shattered. I think it would have been easier had his reasons been he did not like the color of my hair or my five foot nearly nine inch height. For to hear the stabbing words, "you have too many kids" shot through me like an arrow laced with deadly poison. I realized I was nothing more than a burden to society, a burden few wanted to carry.

Tom's visitation weekends continued as regular as clockwork. Every other Friday, he picked the children up at five then brought them home Sunday evening. We spoke very little to each other. Now that our divorce was final, he showed no interest in striking up a conversa-

Loving and happy at home.

tion. I too, had nothing to say. Most of the time, I smelled alcohol on his breath and could tell by his sometimes obscene behavior that he had been drinking. He'd already picked up two DUI's. I could only hope he no longer smoked pot.

These latest hopes of Tom living some sort of half-way decent lifestyle crashed to the earth one day when a great *revelation* came from out of the sky—literally. While the children played tag at the park on a lazy Sunday afternoon, romping around on slides and monkey bars, a strong breeze brought the clear, definite odor of marijuana. "Hey Mommy," Matthew yelled out to me, "that smells like daddy's bathroom." *Out of the mouth of babes.* Yet, I felt helpless to do a thing about Tom's habits. *I can pray* I told myself, *pray for their protection.* As year one of visitation ended, that's exactly what I continued to do.

One evening, at a church worship service, a man named Chris approached me and introduced himself. There hadn't been room in my life for dating, and with four youngsters trailing my very shadow, the guys weren't exactly lined up at the door. Since Martin, I had barely even chatted with a single man. Chris was clearly interested, and I felt flattered. And I think loneliness was written all over my face.

Chris and I had a lot in common, which attracted me to him even more. He had a degree in journalism, was in the middle of writing his first novel, and he liked country living. I saw only one problem, one which became increasingly apparent the more we got to know each other. Chris was a free spirit, one who I could honestly not see raising and supporting a family. Though well-educated, he had never held regular employment and lived a bare subsistence type existence.

Ignoring these warning signs, I continued seeing him on the weekends that my kids were away. As we fell in love, I hoped that love might motivate him to change. Chris and I grew close quickly, going from friends to much more all too soon. Because of this we decided to break it off for awhile, but I was miserable without him, and he confessed, he was too. We got back together then broke up again. This went on for several months. Apart more than we were together, I either anguished from being away from him or felt guilt-ridden for being too physically involved when we were together.

I began to resent my beliefs, blaming them for my predicament. I believed in sexual purity for the Christian single, yet now that I'd met someone, I found it torment to live it. With so many children, I knew that marriage to Chris was unlikely. And by now I had convinced myself there would never be anyone else. When alone, I could more easily stuff passion and desire in some back recess of my mind, but now they seemed to control me rather than I controlling them.

It frightened me to see how vulnerable I really was. When I thought I was so strong, in actuality I was weak. I felt distraught, realizing I had ventured onto a dead-end road, one that could possibly lead to a spiritually dangerous cliff. The longer I dallied in this relationship, the less clear my vision for the future became. I saw only years of solitude.

As a product of the hippie generation where free love was the *in thing*, I felt the permanent scars on my life. Having given away my virginity at the age of seventeen to a boy I thought I'd marry, heart-rendering disappointment filled my life when I discovered nothing but pain and heartache.

At age twenty-eight I still unconsciously sought for that seemingly unattainable human love, though I desperately wanted to do it God's way. The Spirit within vehemently challenged me to do it God's way, allowing me to experience an inconsolable agony of separation from God if I dared to do it any other way.

Finally, after my fourth break-up with Chris, I cried out to God with all of my heart to help me do the right thing. Knowing deep inside that God did not want us together, that our relationship brought no glory to God, I also knew that in and of myself I didn't have the strength to say good-bye only to be left alone again. With the children away at their dad's one November afternoon, the house quiet, I prayed until the late autumn sun settled low enough to leave the room dancing with dim rays of golden light. Then, as He had so often done in the past, the Lord spoke through a scripture, one in II Corinthians that I was familiar with, "My grace is sufficient for you, for My strength is made perfect in weakness." A tranquility which hadn't been there before permeated my soul.

It seems God knows our character, who we are and what we are made of. After all, He created us and knew us before the foundation of the world. Though failures are miserable marks in our lives which set us back, God is looking at the whole picture, and His desire is to refine us into that beautiful bride of Christ. Through our failures, He allows us to see our utter wretchedness and our deep need for a Savior.

For the next two weeks, my energy focused entirely on the Lord, thanking Him for His strength and His forgiveness. My desire to restart the relationship up again with Chris was at last gone, and I saw clearly the true frailty of mankind in myself, and that except for the grace of God, we cannot live the way He wants us to. The Lord spoke to me through Psalm 51, David's prayer of repentance after his affair with Bathsheba. As I read that Psalm over and over, it felt like ointment on an open wound, "Create in me a clean heart, O God, and renew a steadfast spirit within me. Do not cast me away from Your presence, and do not take Your Holy Spirit from me. Restore to me the joy of Your salvation and uphold me by Your generous Spirit" (vs.10-12).

Joy and peace became my friends again when once more the beauty of God's presence overflowed in my life. My loving Father assured me that He is quick to welcome His children with open arms. When we sin, it is like a dark tunnel—dismal, scary, with no way out. When we repent and return to him, it is like a bright, warm spring day with gentle breezes and sweet aromas, cleansing us inside and out.

Nearly three weeks after the blessed afternoon of surrender, I started waking up each morning feeling sick. At first, I could hardly believe God would let such a disaster happen. *Why would you let me get pregnant again when I have already gone through so much and tried so hard to be good all these years?* Though I blamed no one but myself, I couldn't understand why God didn't intervene.

How will I face everyone, my children, my parents, and here I am, a Christian, a single mom? This wasn't the kind of situation someone could hide. I could have gotten drunk, and no one might have known that. Maybe I could have robbed a bank and not been caught, but this, the whole world was going to know.

Two months later, after I waited as long as I could to break the news, I decided to tell my pastor. Perspiration clung to my hands as I sat across from Pastor Jon. As the words began spilling out, his face and eyes softened. Sensing my disgrace and shame, he spoke. "Catherine, I have a scripture for you." We turned together to Genesis 50, in which unfolded the story of Joseph who had been sold by his brothers to the Egyptians. Years later when he was reunited to his betraying now remorseful siblings, they saw no way their brother could forgive them. Joseph comforted them, saying, "Do not be afraid ... you meant evil against me; but God meant it for good." And this, Jon said, was what God wanted me to know, that though Satan began with a sinful plan of destruction, God was going to turn it into good giving me a beautiful child as a reminder of His wonderful grace and love.

Not everyone thought this way about my situation though. As I sat in my college counselor's office, waiting for him to get off the phone, my hands felt clammy, and my heart raced. Trying to get my mind off the reason I came to him, I studied the various book titles on the shelves. Handbooks, manuals, and textbooks covered every aspect of college. I wondered if a book existed that offered help for *my* problem—I doubted it.

Interrupting my thoughts, Mr. Edwards placed the phone on the receiver and leaned forward in his chair, "What can I do for you today, Catherine?"

"I have to drop out of school," I answered.

"Why would you need to do that?" my counselor asked. "You're doing so well in all of your classes."

"I know. I love school, but I, I, ... well I'm pregnant." There, the shocking words were out. I hadn't mustered up the courage to let the world know about this yet, but now, at nearly five months pregnant, I couldn't keep it a secret any longer.

"You don't have to quit school, you know. There *are* other alternatives. What about the father? Is he going to marry you?"

"No." I knew my counselor was anything but a Christian. In fact, he had a reputation for being one of the most liberal professors on campus. Now, I felt my sin would mar his view of Christianity. With my shame, I wanted to run and hide.

"There is really only one thing you can do," Mr. Edwards continued. "Anything else would be unfair to your children and to yourself. You need to have an abortion." The words hit me hard like a slap across the face. I lowered my eyes and shook my head.

"I can't do that."

"Well," he said intently. "If you don't, you will be ruining your life, and it is a very selfish thing to do to your kids. How can you possibly consider having another child?" I thought for a moment and knew in some ways he was right. Raising four children alone was already an insurmountable task. I could barely keep up with everything now, and I was always struggling for more time with the children.

As I listened to his reasons for my having an abortion, my mind drifted back to eleven years earlier...

I was eighteen and one day, I discovered I was pregnant!

"Mom, I need to talk to you." I called my mother, not knowing what else to do. "I'm pregnant."

"You're going to have an abortion, aren't you?"

"I guess." I was surprised my mother knew about such things. It was 1973, and few people discussed abortion.

It all happened so fast. I arrived at the hospital early one morning. A nurse took me to a room, gave me a gown and then a shot to make me drowsy. Soon an attendant wheeled me to an operating room, and I remembered nothing more. When I woke up, it was over. They said they did a D & C abortion. I didn't even know what that meant, and no one explained a thing.

Not until three years later, after I had become a Christian did the full impact of what I had done hit me. I then realized, I had killed my baby. I cried and cried and begged God to forgive me. And somehow I felt I had been robbed. "Why hadn't someone told me, just once, 'Are you sure you want to murder your baby?' Had someone actually spoken those words, I wonder today if I would have done it. And now here I was, so many years later being told by a college professor to have an abortion. Only this time, I knew exactly what it meant!

I stood up to leave the professor's office. "Mr. Edwards, thank you for your concern. But I cannot kill my baby to make *my* life easier. I do not have the right to take the life of another human being." He looked at me but never said another word.

As I stood outside, looking across the campus, an early spring breeze brushed gently across my face. I thought I could smell lilacs in the air. And then it happened. I felt my baby kick. It was as if this unborn child knew what had just happened and rejoiced that I had chosen to keep her, rejoiced that I had chosen life.

The months passed as the children endured my nutritional experiments with tofu, homemade soymilk, and alfalfa sprouts. When summer arrived, we frolicked in the nearby river as we watched in repeated wonder just how big a woman's stomach could get.

In August, on a hot summer afternoon, with my friend Wendy and my mother at my side, Emily Michelle was born weighing ten pounds, one ounce! It was a tough delivery, but one look at her and I could only feel joy.

At home, she became the delight of our lives. The kids were as thrilled as I to have a beautiful new baby. No doubt about it, God knew how to bring good out of chaos and sin.

Just before the birth of Emily, Tom was scheduled to take the children to Kansas for three weeks as he had done also the summer before. As an act of kindness, I offered to clean his apartment while they vacationed. Though later it would be questioned as to my motive for that offer, only one thing entered my mind—making life a bit nicer for my kids.

Walking through his apartment appalled me to see the filth and lack of lighting and furniture. The girls had been sleeping on two mattresses in one of the bedrooms while the boys apparently slept on the floor beside them. The second bedroom was filled with Tom's tools along with boxes of all kinds of junk. This, I decided, should be the girl's room.

As I shoved items into the closet, one of the boxes I picked up off the floor slipped out of my arms, fell to the floor and broke open. There before my eyes, scattered all over the rug, lay piles of filthy pornographic magazines. I picked one up, opened it then slammed it shut. Quickly, I stuffed them into a paper bag and put them on the highest shelf in the closet. After cleaning the entire apartment, throwing away piles of marijuana seeds and beer bottles, I wrote Tom a lengthy letter for him to read when he returned. I advised him that how he lived was none of my business, but he could at least try to *act* decently when the kids were around. I told him I'd found the magazines and how dare he leave them where the boys might see them. While I placed the letter on his television, I doubted it would do much good. The thought of my children being in such an environment tormented me.

When the kids arrived home three weeks later, I asked them if they had ever seen any bad magazines at their dad's place. "We have never seen anything like that, Mom," each of them assured me. Relieved that I had evidently gotten things picked up in time, I appealed to God for my children's safety from anything evil. I constantly worried about the effects Tom's drinking, pot smoking and now reading matter would have on them.

One Sunday evening, several months later, I picked the kids up from Tom's. The girls seemed agitated as they sat in the back seat of our car. "What's wrong, girls?" I queried, glancing at them through the rear view mirror. "Is something wrong?"

"Oh nothing Mama," they both said in unison. "It's just that dad took us over to his boss' house to spend the night," Sarah added. My heart skipped a beat. I thought maybe other kids had been there, and one of them had been unkind to the girls. Without wanting to sound anxious, I asked calmly,

"Well did anyone hurt you? Were there other kids there?"

"Only his two daughters. There was just a lot of swearing and drinking. We don't like it over there." When I got home, after putting the kids to bed, I called my ex-husband. I was furious and determined to let him know.

"Tom, where did you take the kids this weekend?" I demanded.

"We went to my boss' place; had some work to do there." He spoke quietly and politely, which was not his custom. Tom was no longer the quiet guy I once knew. He was often loud and obnoxious, something I attributed to his years of heavy drinking, pot smoking and his father's influence.

"Listen to me, Tom. Don't you ever take those kids to spend the night at anyone's house again. They come to stay with *you*, not with other people. I don't know what went on there, but I'm sure it wasn't good."

"Oh sure, Catherine, never again." He must have been shaking in his boots. I wonder now if the girls were hoping that night I would have pried further until I found out what really happened … If only I'd read more into things, if only I could have seen. However, it never crossed my mind. Tom never took the kids near his boss' house again, and the girls never talked about that weekend anymore.

I felt very fortunate to have such loving children. They were kind to people and to each other. My little brood had grown to five, with the oldest not yet ten. No doubt, we were quite a sight to see every Saturday morning as we did our weekly grocery shopping.

It never occurred to me why they were so protective of each other and me. Once, when I dropped the kids off at Tom's, I had come into the kitchen for a drink of water. Tom, who'd been drinking, grabbed my arm then slurred, "Catherine—these kids need a full time father." I tried pulling away but he wouldn't let go. Suddenly, Matthew ran up and fiercely started kicking Tom, a look of terror in Matthew's young eyes.

"Leave my mom alone," he shouted. Tom let go of me, laughing as he walked away. Such an incident never happened again. I left the apartment surprised at both Tom's boldness and Matthew's fervent four-year-old attack. I never once wondered why the children liked our home so much, never thought it was their refuge from the assaulting storm. Perhaps if they had known Psalm 55, they would have been reciting it when darkness fell each night at their dad's:

Oh, that I had wings like a dove! I would fly away and be at rest.
Indeed, I would wander far off, and remain in the wilderness; I would
hasten my escape from the windy storm and tempest. (vs.6,7)

One morning in April, during my devotions, the Lord gave me a
word from Luke 22 that Satan was going to sift my life like wheat. It
seemed a strange message for God to say to me, especially when it
already felt like I was being sifted—the stresses of raising five children alone, always trying to figure out how to pay the bills, worrying
about Tom, having our old car constantly break down. No, it seemed
like this had already happened in my life. *How could things possibly
become more difficult, and how could I possibly muster up any more strength?* In
addition, my dream for a kind, godly husband sure didn't look prom-
ising. *If the single guys at church were afraid to come near me when I had four
kids, they must be terrified now with five*, I reasoned.

One spring morning, a month after that peculiar word, while
traveling across town with Peter and Emily, we were hit by an on-
coming car. Only seconds before I noticed Peter's seat belt was off,
and I told him to fasten it up. It was no less than a miracle when he
did it so quickly. He was four years old. Emily and he were unhurt,
but our car was totaled. We were taken in an ambulance for injuries

I had sustained, which included a concussion and a slashed arm.

It took several weeks for me to recuperate from the accident. My arm and shoulder were out of commission temporarily while I endured horrible headaches from the head injury. I suffered from some kind of temporary nerve damage to my left leg, and for days my face looked like I'd been in the ring with George Foreman.

When summer reached Oregon and I had for the most part recovered from the accident, I remembered the scripture that God had spoken to me in April. *Ah-ha, God must have* been *warning me about the accident.* It was true; I had suffered a great deal of pain during those two months. *Yep, that must be what God meant.*

I found myself more easily stressed out after the accident and was having a frustrating time coping with all of the responsibilities. I cried easily, sometimes speaking sharply to the kids. And so, when June rolled around and they left for their three weeks in Kansas, I felt a twinge of relief to be left alone. *Besides, at least in Kansas they are with their grandmother who will feed and take care of them properly,* and I seriously doubted Tom would be smoking pot in his parents' home.

The time alone with just the baby was a well-needed time of rest and inner reflection. I headed for our favorite spot in the whole world—a Christian family camp nestled in the foothills of the Cascade Mountain Range. A kind of heaven on earth place for the children and I, we had frequented its doorsteps since 1976. We knew the owners well, and in spite of our inability to pay much, they always made us feel welcome and at home. Without exception, God always did some work in my heart whenever I went.

This particular visit would become a turning point in my family's future. While there, I read a book by Catherine Marshall, the wife of the late Peter Marshall. She had recently become one of my favorite authors as she expounded on the secret of the Christian life being a life of surrender and relinquishment to God. She also believed, as I discovered that day, a Biblical Old Testament law stating that the sins of the fathers shall be passed on from generation to generation.

As I drank in the fragrance of evergreen trees and fresh clear

Cascade air, I thought about my ex-husband's family. There was something inauspicious about them; I knew this, sensed this, but I couldn't name it. Something about Tom, about his parents, was going to affect my children if I didn't start fighting against it. My best guess—it was alcohol. Tom was an alcoholic, and I suspected Ralph was too.

That very day, I began praying in a way I never had before. Boldly denouncing any influence that unknown sins in the Crawford family might have on my children's lives, I pleaded the blood of Jesus over them concerning this matter. I felt so strongly I must fight this unknown thing with more serious, more aggressive prayers. The law of the land said there was nothing I could do to protect my children; God's eternal law said there was.

When I returned from my sanctuary in the mountains, still having a few days left before the kids would be home, I decided to clean Tom's apartment again as I had done so the previous summer. He had left me his key, hoping I would go.

The place looked little better than it had a year ago, except now the girls did have their own room. Tom's tools were cluttered all over their room though, so I decided to organize the closet in order to make more room for his stuff. As I sorted through the dusty closet, I spotted a stack of magazines on the top shelf. I immediately recognized them as the pile of pornographic magazines I'd come across the summer before. Seeing them there again, I became furious. *How can I allow my children to keep coming over here when I know Tom is getting high, drinking and looking at such filth!* I grabbed the large pile of pornography, stuffed them into a box, then carried the box outside to the dumpster.

I gave out a sigh of relief as I tossed them into the pile of garbage. It felt great to be taking some action. If nothing else, my unyielding prayers had at least given me some gumption to take a stand. *And* I would talk to Tom and tell him, he'd better clean up his life.

After picking up the kids from his place a few nights later and getting them to sleep, I dialed his number. My stomach churned with anxiety as I expected him to be mad about the magazines. "Tom"

I began. "I found your magazines again. Well, I threw them away."

"Oh man, those didn't belong to me. They were my boss' and they're worth a lot of money." *Yah, I bet they are,* I sarcastically thought.

"Well that's too bad, Tom. Have your boss call me. I'll be happy to tell him what I told you." My fear in confronting Tom was being replaced by boldness and indignation. "Those magazines are vile, and I don't want the kids around them!" He never raised his voice in anger as I had expected. Rather, he sounded anxious and nervous.

The children were tired and worn out after that trip. They were glad to get home, saying over and over how much they missed me. I too had missed them.

"I don't think they had a good time this year," I wrote in my journal that night. "Tom drank, and I suspected from how he was acting tonight, he was drinking while driving. I must keep the children from going over there until he seeks professional help. Lord please give me the guidance. The children are sugared out, overweight and seem nervous. Still, with a little natural food, lots of prayer and love, they'll be back to normal in a few days … bless their hearts. I missed them so. Little eyes, I think you've seen too much of this sinful ol' world…" I had no idea then just how prophetic those words of verse were. The sifting of my life had not even begun. My prayers had been ascending to heaven; God was about to crash in on hell itself.

Five

Secrecy Broken

Enough

May kids be brave enough to tell
Mothers be strong enough to believe
The Church, Christ-like enough to support
America, wise enough to judge
May offenders be sorry enough to stop.

Slowly I dialed my ex-husband's number. The children had been home from their vacation for a few weeks, and I had finally built up the nerve to give Tom an ultimatum about his destructive behavior. He listened quietly at first. However, when I told him the time had come for him to take his responsibilities seriously and that maybe I wouldn't let the kids come over until he changed, he abruptly stopped me. Speaking in a cold, loud voice, he said, "Don't ever try to keep those kids from me. You'll be sorry if you ever do."

Tom's threat sounded more like Ralph's words than his own. Though I'd never admit it to Tom, I was afraid of them both.

"Well, you better not bring any more of those magazines into your place, and stop drinking and smoking pot when the kids are over." My plans to deliver a life-changing warning had been thwarted. He took it with a grain of salt. But what could I do? His addictions had not visibly hurt the kids by legal standards. My only recourse was to pray for God's shelter and that Tom would either change his ways or go away. *These cannot be ordinary prayers though*, I reasoned.

"Not by might, nor by power, but by My Spirit," says the Lord.

Summer burned at its peak with temperatures soaring well into the high nineties. We moved out of a now crowded two bedroom manufactured home that I had purchased a couple years earlier into

a century old, two story house. Emily was almost one, Peter was four, Matthew six, Rachael eight, and Sarah had just turned ten. Life progressed with much effort. There was never enough money, always too much work and certainly too few hours of sleep. Yet not once did I ever

Emily - A Gift From God

regret being the mother of any of my children. They were considerate, loving, respectful and honest, and they rarely fought or squabbled among themselves. A stampeding herd of antelope possessed less energy than they, mind you. Enthusiastically, they often created productions which included many cheery songs. Using pots and pans with an old guitar, they sang and danced all the while searching for signs of my unsurprising approval.

When the stress of unpaid bills or a broken down car overwhelmed me, when the strain of carrying the heavy burden became too unbearable, they came to the rescue like a life boat to a drowning sea captain. Offerings included homemade cards of many colors, each of them signed with scribbly names and sweet affections. "You're the best mom in the whole world," they chorused together. The children reminded me that the importance and goodness of life wasn't contained in the visible world of cars and bills but more so in the unseen, untangible things like love and devotion.

For the past three years, Tom's visits had included nothing

more than what the law legally obliged me to give—two weekends a month, three weeks in the summer. He rarely missed a weekend due him but never had them extra days. An ex-husband could be a convenient babysitter, but I would have thought it a betrayal of soul, likening myself to Esau in the Bible who sold his natural birthright for a pot of stew.

*   *   *   *   *

August 17th began like so many other mid-summer days. Already, by early morning, the heat slipped without ado into the valley. Before the day ended, thermometers would be reading nearly a hundred. Having been in our new house for less than a week, there were boxes to unpack, dishes to put away and laundry laying everywhere needing to be folded. I spent the better part of the day cleaning, organizing and trying to turn the house into a home. I hung my wooden-framed, embroidered picture, "Home Is Where The Heart Is," in a specially chosen spot on the living room wall. "No matter where we live," I often told the kids, "we're at home as long as we're together." Soon, we would have familiar pictures hanging, flowers growing in the yard, probably next to a small vegetable garden, and this rented house would be called our home.

When we finished dinner that evening, it was still early with ample daylight hours remaining. After finishing the dishes, wiping off the counters and sweeping the floor, I rested on the steps of the big front porch watching the kids play in the sprinkler. "Hey guys," I called out. "Maybe I'll see if I can borrow twenty dollars from your dad tonight. We'll go to the store and buy some rakes, maybe more garden hose." The idea just popped in my head from out of nowhere. Tom had always paid a small amount of child support each month, and on occasion helped with the kids' school tuition or gasoline for the car. Only those were usually planned payments and not any spur of the moment requests like this.

The girls jumped up and down thinking my idea sounded great. As I headed inside to the telephone, they all grabbed their towels and followed me, talking about all the things we would buy with the twenty dollars (more like a thousand in *kid* dollars). The girls ordered the boys to run and put on clean clothes as they plopped their damp selves down on the couch next to me.

"Sure you can have some money for that," Tom said, sounding more than agreeable. "If you want, you can take my Visa card and spend fifty dollars. You probably don't want to go shopping with all the kids. Why don't you drop them off? You can leave the baby too." It wasn't the first time Tom had offered to keep little Emily. *No way*, I always thought to myself, *at least I do have some control over where she goes.*

"Thanks," I answered. "But the girls want to go shopping. I guess the boys might want to come over."

"Let me talk to Matthew," Tom said. Matthew listened while his father talked to him then excitedly said, "Okay, bye Dad." His dad had promised to buy him and his brother some candy if they came over. Later looking back, how I wished I'd given more candy, keeping it from being such a specialty in my children's lives. We dropped the boys off at seven. Tom had been drinking. Rather than make a big deal about it, upsetting everyone, the girls and I left, but I made a mental note never to do this again.

Just-girl time was a rare commodity in our boy-filled lives. For two hours we glided through the stores, buying some things, eyeing others. We saw this as a treasured nugget and hoped to hang onto the memory of it always. The baby giggled cheerfully in her yellow sunbonnet and matching summer dress that I had sewn. We bought a garden hose, sprinklers, curtain rods and an array of household useries. After spending the fifty dollars allowed us, spending it nearly to the very penny, we gobbled up frozen yogurt cones, then arrived back at Tom's apartment a few minutes past nine.

The western sky broke into a dazzling red as the sun began to slip behind the summer-browned hills as if saying to all, "Catch me if you can." Tom and the boys were playing in the parking lot; Peter ran wildly in circles. *Uh-oh, sugared out*, I guessed. I corralled the boys into the car, Matthew in the back between the girls, Peter in the front with the baby. As I thanked Tom for his help, I noticed his garbled speech, and he seemed to be acting peculiar (more than usual anyway). The thought crossed my mind that maybe he was this drunk every time he had the kids but sobered up by the time Sunday evening rolled around when I usually saw him. But on this hot summer night, his intoxication level appeared higher than usual.

Tom became a constant substance abuser early in his life. He began drinking hard liquor and smoking cigarettes at ten-years old. As an adult, Tom couldn't merely have a drink or a cigarette. He smoked three packs of unfiltered cigarettes a day and could easily drink a couple six packs of beer in a few hours. He never smoked just one joint but would have to finish off an entire ounce of marijuana in one sitting. He existed in a state of as much insobriety as humanly possible.

I started getting into my car when he blurted out, "Are you giving Matthew enough baths?"

"Enough baths?!" I responded, squinting my eyes in puzzlement. *What an odd thing to ask.* "Why of course. He takes one almost every night." It was true that in the summer I bathed the kids a little less frequently as they were either running through the sprinklers, playing in our kid-sized pool or at the river on the weekends. "Why?" I asked still holding the door handle.

"He's got a rash on his crotch."

"Well," I said, lowering my voice so the kids couldn't hear, "he doesn't always wipe real well; it could be from that."

"No, it's not on his rear. It's on his crotch."

"Well, I don't have any idea Tom. But I can tell you, he takes plenty of baths." As we drove off, I felt an edge of irritation. *For goodness sake, is he trying to tell me the kids aren't clean?* That was one thing I was always sure of, and Tom knew it.

"Matthew," I asked, looking at my son through the rear view mirror as I drove away, "did you tell your dad you don't take enough baths?"

"No, but sometimes he rubs me there." The words just seemed to roll out, smoothly, as if he told me about some menial task his father does around the apartment. The words rolled out smoothly from Matthew's lips, but they hit my ears sharp and severe. My heart jumped a beat. "He rubs you? Where does he rub you?"

"On my, my privates," he said in a quieter tone. I turned around and looked intently at my son. He sat quietly in between the girls who displayed no reaction but stared blankly at me.

"Sarah, Rachael, do you know anything about this?"

"No Mama," Sarah answered, calling me the name I liked most but rarely heard from my girls anymore.

"Okay, let's not talk about this right now. We'll talk more at home." I had to think. I couldn't though. I raced home as quickly as I safely could. What was only a ten-minute drive seemed to take forever.

When we got in the door, I sent the girls upstairs to get their pajamas on while I fished through a basket of laundry for the boys' pajamas. Sitting on the couch, I buttoned up two sets of red buttons as the girls came scampering down the stairs and plunked themselves down on a large easy chair next to me. *Whatever I do*, I thought, *I mustn't sound alarmed.* So Matthew, can you tell me, has your dad been touching you?"

"Yah."

"Where?"

"Right here," he answered, pointing down at his crotch.

"Do you girls know anything about this; have you seen anything? Sarah?"

"No Mom, I've never seen anything like that."

"Rachael, how about you?"

"Unh-uh," she said, shaking her head

"Why don't you girls take Peter upstairs and read to him while I talk to Matthew?" The baby slept quietly near me on the couch. As they left, I thought it would be better to talk to Matthew alone. I knew from experience with kids that if I wanted to get all the facts in a given story, it could be done a lot more efficiently one on one.

"Matthew, did your dad touch your penis or just between your legs by your penis?" I asked, hoping this was all a misunderstanding and perhaps in some wrestling his dad had accidentally touched him near his genitals.

"He touches my penis."

"How many times did he do that?" I asked, my hands in my lap not daring to move. Matthew shrugged.

Then, "I dunna know." At age six, I knew a child's perception of time and amounts were ambiguous. "When was the first time?"

"Like around Easter," he answered, his sweet little round face looking at me. *Easter*, I thought. *Six months ago.*

"You're a very good boy for telling me Matthew."

"Are you going to tell my dad I told you?"

"I don't know what I'm going to do, but don't worry—everything is going to be all right. I love you, honey."

Later that night, sitting alone in the dimly lit living room, a cool air gently seeped through the slightly open window into the house, finally cooling it down a bit. I pulled my knees to my chest. In a numbing prayer, I asked God to show me what to do. It looked as though I had caught things just in time. This little bit of touching had started maybe six months ago, perhaps Tom had started with Matthew, and that was all. *Thank goodness*, I pondered. *Thank goodness Matthew spoke up.* I figured with all Tom's drinking and pot smoking he had lost his self-control and started this stuff. Though the mere thought disgusted me, I was relieved God had allowed him to be caught before anything worse happened.

The following morning after breakfast, when the kids were already running around outside, my mind felt boggled and unsure of what direction to turn. I knew so little about this kind of thing, not even sure if a crime had been committed. I had a close friend who had been molested by her own father. When she had first told me about her abuse, I was shocked to think that one's natural father would touch his child in a sexual way. Slowly I dialed Janet's number, nearly hanging up at even the idea of having to tell someone, as if telling would bring me out of this bad dream and suddenly make the whole thing real. I could always pretend that nothing happened at all and not tell a soul. Janet's voice interrupted my cowardly thoughts. She listened carefully as I explained what had taken place. "Janet," I asked. "What should I do?"

"No question about it Catherine, what he did is called sexual abuse, and it is against the law. You have got to call the police."

I then made an anonymous telephone call to Children's Protective Services, a state-run child protection service. After explaining what Matthew had told me, they made one comment, "Yes, abuse has occurred, and you need to call the police." I don't know why I didn't run down to the police station that very morning, but I just had to make sure I was doing the right thing. I thought of calling Tom and confronting him but knew that would never work. No one, whether innocent or guilty, is going to listen to someone accuse them of child molesting. One thing I knew without a doubt—Matthew was telling the truth, and I was going to make sure it never happened again.

As the day wore on, I became increasingly worried as I remembered Tom was supposed to have the kids that weekend, which was now just a few days away. I couldn't, I wouldn't let them go. Exactly how to stop the visit, I wasn't sure. The following morning we went down to legal services. Once seated in the attorney's office, I explained to her what had happened and my concerns about the soon coming visitation. "You'll need a restraining order," she said matter-of-factly. They couldn't give me one there, and in fact she said it could take a few days.

"That won't work," I anxiously answered.

"No it won't, but this will." And at that, she picked up the telephone, then placed a call to the courthouse. Within thirty minutes I sat in the judge's private chambers explaining the situation. He signed a restraining order, handed it to me, and with a gentle smile on his face advised me with parting words,

"You will go to the police about this, right?" I later learned everyone's concern that I *wouldn't* report this stemmed from the fact that many mothers don't.

On Friday I awoke early, feeling as if I hadn't slept at all. Though I now had a restraining order, Tom still knew nothing of the kettle that was about to boil over.

That afternoon, after being advised by a friend to do so, we found ourselves sitting in the waiting room of a local professional counseling center. They had agreed to see us immediately. A kids corner filled with toys and books caught the children's eyes, which they lickety-split made their way over to. I sat down in a nearby chair and took in the scope of the room. Pamphlets on sex abuse, physical abuse, eating disorders, mental disorders, all kinds of disorders were stacked neatly on shelves. A handful of people also waited, most of them looking tired and sad. I wondered what brought each of them there, what tragedy had emerged from their lives, and I wished *we* were somewhere else.

The screening counselor was a large, stately woman with short-cropped hair and nearly a smile on her stern, business-like face. While the kids went into her special *playroom*, she and I talked. She then called Matthew into the office and asked me to leave. I said no. Wild horses could not have gotten me to leave my little boy alone with a stranger at that point. I sat quietly as she asked Matthew to explain what he told me. When they finished, she had him join the other kids. "I believe your son is telling the truth and that your ex-husband has sexually abused him. It is our legal duty to inform the police about this abuse. Will you be going to the police yourself?"

"Yes, I guess so ... One more thing though," I said, "I'm concerned that maybe something happened to the girls. They say nothing has, but I don't know. Can you speak with them and tell me what you think?"

"Yes, of course." While Peter, Matthew and I waited in her counseling room, she joined the girls in the playroom. Fifteen minutes later she reappeared. "I think it's fairly safe to say the girls have not been abused." Later I found out she used the fifteen minutes to simply observe the girls playing with a dollhouse, some doll dishes and a couple dolls. Never once did she ask them, "Did your dad touch you in a bad way?" or "Did he abuse you in any way?"

As we left the counseling center, I glanced at my watch—it was just after five, Friday afternoon. I called Tom and told him the kids had come down with a terrible flu, so we had better postpone his visit. Though so afraid he would suspect some queer thing in my voice, he cheerfully, probably drunkenly said, "No problem."

There is really nothing left to do but turn him in, I told myself. *Did he think Matthew wouldn't tell—as close as my kids are to me, how could he think that?* I drove slowly down Central Street towards the police station, still hoping for something short of a miracle.

Carrying Emily in one arm, holding Peter's hand with the other, I beckoned the girls and Matthew to follow behind as we walked up the steps of the police station. "I need to report a crime," I told the woman behind the window inside.

"What is the crime?" she requested.

"Sex abuse."

"Wait outside over there by that bench," the receptionist ordered. The officer we would talk to was on his way in from the streets, she told us. For the kids, who had been cooped up most of the afternoon, the tree-lined courtyard offered a welcome change. Though quieter and more subdued than usual, they ran around like a bunch of little puppies. Minutes later a tall, robust-looking officer made his way up from the parking lot. Glancing towards me, he wore no smile on his square-jawed face, and I guessed he had to deal with this stuff all the time.

"What can I do for you, ma'am?" he sternly inquired moments later as he stood towering over me.

"I think my ex-husband has been molesting my son."

"And what makes you think that?" I hinted sarcasm in his voice. *He doesn't believe me,* I assumed. *Probably thinks I'm just another woman who hates her ex-husband.*

"Because he told me; my son told me."

"Where is he now?" he asked, evidently not seeing the kids yet. I called Matthew over, and they all came running.

"These are *all* your kids?"

"Yes. This is Matthew." The officer introduced himself, then sent all but Matthew back to play. His voice still carried an intimidating sternness. Negative feelings about this guy filtered through my head. *Here's this big, young, handsome cop. He probably has a perfect life, gorgeous wife, great house and car. And here I am, some single mother with worn jeans, five kids—noisy ones, and my old Rambler station wagon. I'm sitting here reporting my ex for sex abuse.* I just knew he thought he had me all figured out.

"Well son, can you tell me what you told your mom?" The officer knelt down allowing his 6'3" body to match this little boy's size.

"Uh, my dad, he touched me down there," Matthew said pointing to his crotch.

"What is that called, Matthew? You like to be called Matthew?"

"Yah, Matthew."

"What's that called where you pointed?"

"My penis," he whispered.

"Your penis?" the officer answered back. "You don't have to whisper that word, Matthew. It's okay to say penis. He ruffled Matthew's hair, looked up at me and smiled. He no longer had the harsh, judging glare in his eyes.

"I need to take a tape recorded report down of what Matthew has said; I'd like to have you stay out here while I take him inside."

"I'd really like to be with him, but if he's willing to go, I guess it's okay with me."

"How 'bout it bud? Can you go with me and help me out?"

"Okay," Matthew responded without reservation, taking Officer Johnson's hand. Twenty minutes later they re-emerged. Matthew scooted off to play with the others.

"I have no doubt in my mind Matthew is telling the truth. Your ex-husband has sexually assaulted him. We're going right over to arrest him." The words, spoken as normal everyday words to him, seemed to me so final, so sure.

I had hoped someone would say, "No, I think Matthew is mistaken—this didn't really happen." No one uttered such words though, and I had no remorse for turning Tom in. He had messed up, and he'd been caught. "What about the other kids? Have you asked them if anything happened to them?"

"I've asked. Peter and Rachael seem hesitant; Sarah says nothing happened to her. Just Matthew, I think, that's all."

"Well, I hope so."

Two hours later, after we'd finished dinner and sat quietly watching a television show, the telephone rang. "This is Officer Johnson. We arrested Tom Crawford on a felony charge of sex abuse. He'll be lodged in the county jail tonight, but I should warn you. I think his dad is going to get him out on bail. He called Kansas—Tom was crying—sounded scared and very upset. I don't know what he'll do when he gets out. Is there a place you can go for the weekend?" … *Yes, that's what we'll do,* I thought. *Tom will be mad.* I called my old friend, Carol, who lived a hundred miles north of us. Without hesitation, she told us to get in the car—of course we could stay.

Battling the pursuing images that tried taking over my mind, my being, I hastily packed bags for our two-day evasion—evasion from a man I was angry at, a man I was afraid of. Near midnight we wearily pulled into Carol's driveway. Tip-toeing into the darkened house, we piled into already prepared beds and sleeping bags. The children fell straight to sleep, but for me rest was a distant stranger.

Tom was out of jail by the following morning. Sure enough, his father had posted bail and rescued his son as he had many times before for drunk driving charges. On Sunday, Ralph called my father. My parents had moved from California a few years earlier and now lived close to the children and me. Ralph talked to my dad and tried to strike a deal. He insisted Tom would leave Oregon, never to return again, if we would drop all the charges. "Such a tempting thought," I told my father. If Tom left, I could be guaranteed he would never hurt the kids again.

However, when we returned home on Monday morning, I soon learned it didn't matter what *I* wanted to do. The State of Oregon was pressing charges, and it wasn't up to me to keep or drop them. Nevertheless, I revisited Legal Services at which time the attorney drew up a document for Tom to sign. He had agreed to sign this paper, and in fact, his father initiated the idea. However, when he arrived at Legal Services the following day and read the paragraph that made a confession to his touching Matthew, he took the paper with him and left. Ironically, I would later be accused of plotting all of this, everything from Tom leaving the state to signing a confession. On the contrary, I was merely caught in between the plans of others.

By Monday afternoon, Children's Protective Services had been informed, the District Attorney had been informed, and friends and family of both sides had been informed. It looked to authorities like another routine child abuse case. Unbeknownst to all, this was to become the largest, most complicated child sexual abuse case this community had ever witnessed.

That night as the children slept in their beds, I stood in the softly lit hallway just outside their rooms. The only sounds heard were those of the crickets chirping in the grass, singing gloriously of day's end and night's cool beginning. The words of Officer Johnson pulsated repeatedly, haunting me through and through: "I find it hard to believe Matthew is the only one. As a matter of fact, statistics prove that is likely not the case…" Recent comments made by Peter and Rachael left police doubting what I desperately clung to—that Matthew alone had suffered and at that, only mild abuse. The officer's stinging words echoed like yells heard in a mountain-surrounded valley. A formidable coldness ran through me. I climbed into bed and pulled the covers around my neck. A chilly wind blew in through the open window. I shivered then turned my back and closed my eyes.

Stolen Innocence

annie died the other day
never was there such a lay—
whom, among her dollies, dad
first ("don't tell your mother") had;
making annie slightly mad
but very wonderful in bed
saints, satyrs, go your way
youths and maidens, let us pray
e.e.cummings

"It's been nearly a week since I discovered Tom has been sexually molesting Matthew." The words penned in my journal spoke painfully clear: "Nothing, in my entire life, has ever made me feel the way I do right now. Please don't let this hate stay with me forever."

One day, a man from Children's Protective Services came to our house and asked to speak with Matthew. Tall, distinguished looking with a dark beard and a quiet voice, he placed himself on the couch then removed a tape recorder from his briefcase. I sent all but Matthew out to play.

"Would you please leave the room?" he asked me.

"No," I responded as I took a seat in an inconspicuous corner.

Eyeing me carefully, he beckoned Matthew to join him on the couch. He chatted for a moment with my son then said, "You know Matthew. Your dad isn't a bad person. He's just made a mistake." Wham! Words like a strong gusty wind slapping against bare skin landed in my ears.

Am I really hearing this? Who is this man? I stared in disbelief. *All of my life—you do as you are told, obey authority unquestioned, and of course, be respectful towards government, government such as Children's Protective Services who can take away your kids. How can I sit here any longer? When they told me I could do nothing three years ago when I thought Tom was a threat, I said okay. When Tom said no way could I stop him from seeing the kids no matter how he behaved, I backed down. Now, in my living room, with my child, this man will tell my son what's happened is okay, not a big deal. No. This cannot be. Enough is enough. I will protect my children from now on, and no one is going to tell my children things that are not true. No one is going to intimidate me when it comes to my kids anymore. No one is going to tell me I can't sit in the same room with my child, and 'no one' is going to make me or my child listen to this man.*

Like a windmill suddenly stopping and changing direction because new winds overtook it, I jumped to my feet, startling both Matthew and the man. "Please leave my home now!" It was not a request but an order. "This man who you say has made a mistake is a child molester, and you are not going to make it out to be some petty matter. Now please leave. We don't need your help!"

Shortly after that, Rachael and Peter started spilling little bits and pieces of what was to become a horrifying tale. Knowing my kids could never have made such things up, they each shared similar stories yet never heard the other brother or sister talk. I was convinced beyond any doubt. Besides, they had no reason to discredit their father in such a damaging way. As Rachael described a wetness between her legs after Tom did it or the sound of his heavy breathing, I knew she was describing nothing but actual accounts.

The ensuing three weeks were filled with hours of interviews. Matthew, Peter and Rachael, piece by piece, unfolded details of their abuse which went far beyond the realms of a little touching. Each of them had been touched on their genitals numerous times by Tom, and each of them had been made to touch Tom. Usually the abuse occurred at night, after the kids were in bed. Sometimes, in the early evening as they all watched television, Tom would hold one of them on his lap, a blanket covering them both while he fondled their private parts. Their words incriminated this man they called Daddy.

As I learned further details of the abuse, the entries in my journal took on a new tone: "Discouragement has enveloped my soul," I slowly wrote. "I understand more clearly now the words of Job: 'When I looked for good, evil came to me; and when I waited for light, then came darkness. My heart is in turmoil and cannot rest; days of affliction confront me. I go about mourning but not in the sun [without comfort]; I stand up in the assembly and cry out for help' (Job 30:26-28)." My children, the light of my life, had been sexually assaulted.

Now that my three younger children were starting to open up, I found it harder to believe Sarah had not been abused too. Yet I didn't want to press her for information that might not exist. Afraid of influencing the kids in any way, I wanted the truth to come out but nothing more.

On different occasions, I asked Sarah briefly if she was sure nothing had happened between her and her father. Her answer was always the same—nothing happened. Finally, I stopped asking. *Perhaps*, I reasoned, *she is feeling betrayed by me and will resent that she is not believed. As close as Sarah and I have been all her life, surely by this time she would have spoken up.* Still it seemed odd that Sarah never asked any questions about her siblings' abuse. She showed no signs of shock, surprise or curiosity—things I would have expected from someone who knew nothing about these things. She remained completely silent.

Many days passed. We heard little from the District Attorney's office as they laboriously processed arraignments and indictments. As each child spoke up, the police added new charges. The list grew. I didn't cry though—time didn't allow. *I'll do that later*, I told myself. *Right now, I must do everything I can to protect my kids.* Pangs of guilt carved at my soul. *I should have seen the signs*, I told myself over and over.

Then one day, when the initial signs of autumn hung quietly in the air, the kids and I were driving through town doing our food shopping. Stopping for one sale at one store then another sale at another, we made our way through an array of streets and avenues. "Look Mama," Rachael burst out. "There's Dad's apartment."

Oh how stupid of me, I've driven right onto his street. I had intentionally avoided this street for the past several weeks not wanting to upset the kids. I glanced up at the second-story window that marked my ex-husband's apartment. "That's weird," I mumbled. "That doesn't look like Tom's lamp. Maybe he's moved."

"Let's go home and call his landlord," Sarah pleaded with an urgent voice. I could hardly believe he would have left the state before the trial, but I agreed to make the call.

"Yes, he left a few weeks ago; said he was going back to Kansas," the friendly landlord confirmed.

Two days later, as I bathed the baby in the upstairs bathroom, I felt the Lord nudging me to talk to Sarah. I was not unfamiliar with the voice of the Holy Spirit but did not know exactly what to think of this urging. I rose from my kneeling position over the tub, leaned out the open window and called out, "Sarah, can you come up here for a moment?"

"Yah Mom," she yelled up then appeared at the bathroom entrance moments later.

"I want to ask you something." I looked into her bright blue ten-year-old eyes; her blonde hair, now cut in a short shaggy style, clung to her sweet face.

"About Tom?" she asked.

How did she know? Has God been talking to her too? "Yes honey. Did Tom, did he ... molest you?" By now, I had stopped referring to Tom as Daddy. "Real daddies don't do these things," I explained to the children. Sarah looked straight into my eyes, secretly feeling a freedom she didn't have while Tom still lived in town. Where fear had gripped tightly for the preceding five weeks, fear that ... She held the key, the key to release her and her siblings from the secrets which hung like a cloud of death over their lives. Rachael, Matthew and Peter brought me to the door, whispering, "Here, it's in here, but you may only have a peek."

Sarah, the oldest, the one they all looked up to, the one they waited for, watching to see what she would do—she held the key that her mother knew nothing about.

"Yes Mom, he raped me." Making no sound, no gasp, I forced my breathing to remain even. With effort, so much effort, I maintained a plain expression on my face. *I mustn't sound alarmed,* I reminded myself. I knew a lot of touching took place between Tom and the three others and that Tom had ejaculated on Rachael—that was horrifying enough! But surely there hasn't been any kind of intercourse.

"When did it happen?"

"I'm not sure."

She's not sure? That's odd. It must have been within the last six months, I assured myself. "Did it happen more than once?" *Please God let it just be once.*

"Yes."

"More than twice?"

"Yes."

"How many times did it happen?"

"I don't know. Too many times to count."

What? What! "Do you remember the first time it happened?" *Easter time, right?*

"I'm not sure."

"Do you remember how old you were when it first happened?"

"Seven." *What did she say? Seven?! But that's, that's three years ago! That's when Tom first started seeing the kids. Oh my God, this couldn't be! God tell me this isn't so! How...? How could this be?* A picture flashed in my mind, Rachael screaming, hiding in the corner when Tom came to pick them up on his second visit, and I had made her go anyway.

My heart beat in heavy, rapid strokes. I felt like someone was squeezing my lungs, sure I would pass out at any moment. No, I was going to throw up. I could feel the color draining from my face, but I calmly answered, "Oh honey, I'm so glad you told me, so glad. Why don't you go back outside now—we'll talk more later," I said with words I forced from my lips. I needed time, time to think, time to die.

"Okay mama." She threw her arms around my waist. Her

eyes filled with tears that didn't drop. "My heart feels so happy now cause I told you." A peaceful look covered her face instead of the adult-like frown she'd worn for weeks. Like the others, she had been having terrible nightmares, waking up crying. She had insisted nothing had happened, was horrified to break secrecy, secrecy she had been sworn to keep … or else. Now she handed it to me. Like a box with a locked lid and a sign saying, DO NOT OPEN, she handed it to me, to take care of properly. No longer did she and the others have to carry this hidden burden. The weight of concealment was lifted from their tiny shoulders. I would not let them down again. *Her heart she says, is happy…*

"I know honey, me too. Me too." When she left, I sat down on the edge of the tub and cried.

My God, how could this have happened to my children? How could You have allowed this? How did I not see it? My heart raced. I felt like a brick had just been hurled through it. I thought I was nobody's fool, thought I knew what was going on. *But none of that is true—I* ***am*** *a fool. I am the greatest fool of all!*

During a police interview, Sarah described how Tom would come into her room at night, after everyone had gone to bed. He would have consumed several beers over the course of the evening and also smoked marijuana in the bathroom. She described his heavy breathing when he was *doing it*, how afterwards she was wet and it felt as if she'd peed.

"Did you ever cry afterwards? Did you ever cry to yourself?"

"No, but I felt like it."

"Did you want to tell somebody about it?"

"Yes."

"Who did you want to tell?"

"Yes."

"My mom."

"Why did you want to tell her?"

"Because I didn't want it to happen anymore."

"Did you want it to happen anymore?"

"No."

"Did you look forward to it happening?"

"NO!"

"How come you didn't tell your mother?"

"Because my dad said if I told, he would hurt my mom or Rachael." The interviewing ended that night but continued throughout the week. Although the other kids never once heard Sarah's interviews, they knew she was talking, and it seemed to give them the freedom to tell every detail they had sheltered for so long. Every time I thought they'd gotten it all out, they had more to tell. It was as if now that they had broken secrecy, they wanted to tell every detail.

It never occurred to me someone else other than Tom might have been involved; so on the night I sat on the couch with Rachael and asked, "Did Tom ever try anything when you visited in Kansas," nothing could have prepared me for her answer.

"Yah, sometimes … So does Grandpa," referring to her grandfather, Ralph.

"Grandpa? What do you mean, Grandpa?"

"He does that stuff too." The now-familiar tightness around my chest returned. My eight-year-old daughter had just told me her grandfather had been molesting her, yet I was too numb to feel the impact of this statement. My little Rachael, my sweet little Rachael. She had always been more sensitive than the others, felt pain easier, like a little flower, I often thought. Her father, her own father and now her grandfather? With no regard about breaking her spirit, no regard for any of their tiny child spirits?

"What about Sarah, Sarah too, or just you?"

"Her too."

"That's a good girl for telling Mommy." I spoke placidly in an even tone. *You cannot fall apart; you cannot freak out here.* I repeated this continually to myself. Thoughts rushed through my head. I stuffed the rage back somewhere in the recesses of my mind. *No time for losing my sanity; I have to keep my cool.*

"Sarah." I sat on the couch minutes later with my oldest daughter. I wanted to approach this carefully. I knew Rachael spoke the truth. She had no reason to say such things about her grandfather. Still, I needed to know for sure. No one ever suggested he was a part of the scenario. No one had even thought it. "Sarah, I want to ask you something. Did anything happen in Kansas with someone other than Tom?" Sarah looked up at me then looked down, turning her eyes away. With quivering lips, she began to tell me about the abuse which happened on their trips to Kansas, abuse that included her grandfather, sometimes her uncle, once a dog, and ... pictures, lots of pictures. She described how her grandfather had done the same things to her that Tom had done to her. She said they took pictures of these things, pictures of Sarah and Rachael together, of the boys together—my little boys. The pictures had been taken in Oregon by Tom and in Kansas by Ralph and sometimes Tom.

When I asked Sarah if her grandmother knew about any of this, Sarah replied, "I'm pretty sure she knew about it. One time, I saw her looking."

I called the boys, each separately and asked them the same non-leading question. Did anything happen in Kansas? Yes. With whom? Daddy and Grandpa. As the chronicle unfolded, a hazy picture now became clear—the evilness I had always sensed in this family, the feeling something wasn't right. *How in God's name could a grandmother know about such wickedness happening to her own flesh and blood and not do anything to stop it?* In my wildest imagination I could not comprehend it.

"Dad." I called my father that night. "You better sit down. What I have to tell you is going to be a shock." My father is a quiet, modest man. He's worked every day since he was fourteen and in many ways has been sheltered from the vile things of this world. To him, the very *thought* of a father or grandfather molesting their child is nothing less than utterly detestable, as it is for any decent man.

He never doubted anything my children relayed to us, and the mere idea made him sick to his stomach.

During one interview, Rachael talked about an incident that took place at her grandparents' house in Kansas. Everyone had gone out this particular afternoon, everyone except Rachael and her grandfather. "We were staying watching television," Rachael recounted. "And he said come here, and I'll give you some candy. So, I went there, and he, he took me in the bathroom and he, I don't know if he locked the door or not, but he put me in the bathtub, and he pulled down my underwear and he pulled down his."

She described the abuse, details about his body, his breathing. Afterwards, without saying a word, he left her there in the bathtub alone and went to his room. He told her never to tell anyone or she would never see her mother again. Throughout the weeks of interviewing, a sinister, deadly thread intricately wove its way through their abuse—"What did he say (meaning Tom or Ralph) would happen if you told?"

"That I would never see my mom again."

"That they would hurt my mom."

"They said if I told they would take me away, and I would never see my mom again." Repeatedly they told the kids that telling would be a worse thing for them than the abuse itself. Once Tom held up a large butcher knife to Rachael and said,

"Remember, don't ever tell your mom what happened!" More than once he told her if she ever betrayed him, he would kill me. Threats were not the only tactic he used to maintain secrecy. Often he conveyed to them how the things he did were okay and that all fathers did them. He even referred to our beloved show, *Little House on the Prairie*, saying, "Pa did these things with Laura back then." His efforts to convince them nothing bad had happened were well-planned, thought-out devices proven time and again by other molesters to be successful in keeping kids quiet.

Most of the pictures were taken in Kansas, sometimes with a still camera, sometimes with a video camera. At times, pictures were taken with one of the children and one of the men, other times with two of the children together, without clothes on, made to perform various sexual acts. Once, probably when Tom was very drunk, he told the kids of his plans—to "sell the pictures and get a lot of money." Trapped in a world of deviant adults, the children offered little challenge for these offenders to control and manipulate. The motivation was not merely sexual pleasure but also for monetary gain, we discovered, as a story of elaborate child pornography unraveled itself.

"How many pictures were taken?" Officer Johnson asked Sarah once.

"I don't know, lots."

"Twenty?"

"No! Lots."

Six weeks after disclosure began, I felt sure we must have been getting to the end of all that happened. What else could there be? They had experienced nearly every form of sexual abuse possible. For three years, what started out with some touching on the part of their father, escalated to full-blown sex abuse with all the children, their grandfather and uncle, even an occasional viewing by their grandmother. Abuse included acts with grown men, forced acts with each other and one incident in which the men used a dog during video filming. Child pornography was orchestrated into much of the abuse. It wasn't enough they stole my children's youth and their innocence; they wanted to make a profit while they perversely enjoyed themselves.

"There's one thing I haven't told you, Mom," Sarah said. A long, tiring day had ended; she and I sat quietly on the couch talking.

"What is it honey?"

"Do you remember when Tom took us to spend the night at his boss' house?" Yes, I recalled it well. I had called Tom up when I found out they'd spent the night there. The girls seemed upset that night, saying there was a lot of drinking and swearing going on. It was the only time he took them there, and I remembered the night well.

"Tom's boss, Frank, well he did some stuff to me when we went there."

"And that's why you were upset that night?"

"Yeah." Sarah had pulled herself into a ball with her knees tucked up tightly. I put my arms around her, hugging her, then placed a gentle kiss on her forehead. My mind raced back to that evening at least five months ago. I could still see the girls sitting in the back seat of the car. I saw their eyes, their little faces. *Sarah, Rachael, … Rachael? She was upset too.* "What about Rachael, did anything happen to her too?"

"I don't know," Sarah said shrugging. But later when I asked Rachael,

"Is there anyone else who touched you, any one of Tom's friends," she answered,

"Tom's old boss." On a visitation weekend when a father takes his children camping in the woods to experience life in the wilds, Tom took his daughters to this strange man's house and allowed him to violate my babies. Neither girl knew this man, this large, gruff man. With their own incestuous father, they at least knew what to expect, but with this stranger, sheer horror and complete humiliation gripped them. A few pictures were taken that night; perhaps money was exchanged. According to the FBI, Tom may have sold the girls that night, perhaps to pay a debt.

This latest and what was to be the final disclosure, opened a new complex issue for the local authorities. Whereas Ralph would have to be investigated then charged back in Kansas, Frank was a local man. Interviews were taken with the girls. Sarah's abuse occurred in his living room—Rachael's in an attic. The police picked up the girls from school one day and took them to the station. A man drew a composite picture of Frank. Two officers then drove us out of town in an unmarked car so the girls could identify the house they'd been abused at. As we approached a two-story farmhouse, Sarah called out, "That's it! That's where we spent the night." They arrested Frank the following afternoon, booked him on charges of rape and sex abuse and then released him.

When the day for Frank's arraignment arrived, I went to the courthouse. As he entered the room, my eyes narrowed on him as I beheld his tough, almost wild look; I hated him vehemently and wished he were dead. If someone handed me a gun at that moment then whispered, "Shoot!" I may have pulled the trigger, without hesitating. And if there was delay in that fraction of a second, it would only be for one reason, I might be caught and never see my kids again. At the time, I felt that was the only basis for not pulling the trigger.

My hate for these men multiplied rapidly like a fast growing tidal wave ready to break over the shores of an unexpecting beach to do its colossal damage. At night, I laid in bed, imagining one scene repeatedly: I was parked across the street from Tom's house in Kansas, the nice neat house on the maple tree lined road. A bomb sat, hidden inside the house. Only when I was sure the whole family was inside, I ignited the fuse, setting the bomb off, and the entire family would no longer exist.

The police came to our house one day unexpectedly, after they had completed a search of Frank's house. Rachael's story had a problem—his place had no attic. The officer who came that day was not Officer Johnson, whom the children loved and had grown to trust. He was on vacation so Officer Jim filled in. Though he was a gentle man, eventually becoming another ally to the kids, they saw him as a stranger that day. Rachael in particular didn't handle new people well. When Officer Jim told her there wasn't an attic, Rachael retracted all she'd said about Frank, now saying nothing happened with him at all. Sarah maintained her testimony. When the officer left, Rachael and I stood in the middle of the living room floor. I asked her why she changed her story. She whispered to me, "I thought the policeman was Tom, that he changed the way he looked and was going to jump out and get us."

Knowing this man, Frank, lived not more than ten miles away from us bothered me immensely. At least Tom was out of the state now. Tom and Ralph had threatened the kids so many times about hurting or killing me that I nearly believed the threats myself. After all, *I* was the main adult witness in the case. I felt terrified they might get rid of me in order to kidnap the kids. *I*

Matthew - His Kindergarten School Picture One Month After He Told.

would be an easy target, I thought, *a woman alone in a big old house with a bunch of helpless children—yes, not much of a challenge.*

We began receiving prank telephone calls, someone calling, listening for a moment then hanging up. The calls came two or three times a day, and they left me jumpy and nervous. Though I tried to make little of the calls in front of the kids, to them once-trusted adults had been making threats to them for three years. How could they know whether they were going to follow through with them or not? In their young minds, these men not only possessed the capability to hurt us, they now had a motive. Often, I found a couple kids in bed with me by early morning saying they awoke in the middle of the night to bad dreams. I too slept restlessly, listening to noises in the night, sounds in the dark.

One frosty November night, the kids and I were up late watching a movie. It was just turning eleven. Our front door had a large oval paned window in it and sheer lacy curtains hanging over the window. When I heard a car pull into our driveway, I got up to look through the window. A small pickup had pulled up, and two scruffy looking men stepped slowly out of the vehicle. I did not recognize either one. The boys ran to the front window, asking me who the men were. "I don't know, but get away from the window boys." I turned to look at the girls: Rachael had scurried to hide behind a large easy chair, and Sarah's face was as white as snow. The men stood at the bottom of the porch, laughing while one pointed his finger at me. I stood, not taking my eyes off them. "Sarah," I called out. "Call 911. Hurry!" Sarah raced to the telephone before I even finished.

"Please help us," she screamed. "Some men are outside our house—they're trying to get us." Speaking rapidly, she gave out our address. "Please hurry," she cried. By now Sarah was near hysteria. Rachael wailed loudly while Peter and Matthew, who were hiding behind the chair, each held a large piece of firewood, ready to attack at a moment's notice.

"Tell her to get someone here fast," I yelled, near hysteria myself. All the weeks of holding it together, and staying calm disappeared that night. A few minutes later the men strolled back to their pickup, then drove away. The police arrived to a house full of freaked out kids and an ashen faced trembling mom. Soon my father and mother arrived, loaded us up in their car and took us to their home for the night. The following day, I did something I'd never done before—I bought a gun and a handful of bullets. Though I had never touched a gun before in my life, I knew I could not sit around night after night defenseless. *Safe* was no longer a word I comprehended.

Disclosure had finally ended. It had lasted six weeks, but finally the gruesome story was out. Winter briskly raced to our sides. A cold North wind blew strong, taking down the remaining leaves from the old oak tree that grew in our yard. I threw another log into the woodstove in hopes of ridding myself from the chill that had set into my bones. It was four o' clock in the afternoon. As I stood at the foot of the stairs, calling to the children, I held my hand on my back. It ached, and I felt tired and old. "Come on kids," I called. "It's time." Pell mell they came, running one after the next down the stairs, throwing themselves onto the couch. I clicked on the T.V. then squeezed in between them, as we joined together to do what we did every day at four—tune into *Little House on the Prairie*. Laura Ingalls held her father's hand as they strolled through the woods. She and Pa were going fishing—father and daughter, the way it's supposed to be.

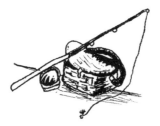

Seven

Sins of the Fathers

Oh where is my youth?
It seems to have fled,
To a far off land
Where rainbows are in every hand.
My heart searches hard,
For something that is gone,
And now my life awaits me,
Beckoning, whispering, calling,
"Lets run away together,
I'll take you by the hand
Back to the land of rainbows
Skimming across the sand."

"Catherine, this is Ken." I recognized the district attorney's voice from the many conversations we'd already had. "You have been ordered by the court to find a professional therapist who can evaluate the kids."

"I'm not going to do it Ken. The kids have been through enough already. They're worn out. I can't believe I am being ordered to do this!"

"Catherine, I understand how you feel. It doesn't seem fair. But if you don't comply, you could be held in contempt of court." I hung up feeling as though the children were being victimized all over again. But since Tom's defense attorney wanted this done, it had to be done.

The FBI became involved with our case because of the child pornography. Federal law states it is illegal to transport children across state lines for immoral purposes. Another law prohibits the manufacturing of child pornography.

My telephone bill soared well over two hundred dollars a month as I began making calls all across the country. I spoke with several FBI agents who handled crimes concerning child pornography. More than once, agents told me if I sent them a picture of my kids, they might be able to find their photos in confiscated materials. If pornographic photos of them *were* located, they could be used for evidence which in turn could mean the children might not have to testify at a trial. In addition, it might implicate all the men at the same time, bringing a definite conviction. Local authorities promised me if a jury convicted Tom for *any* of the charges, he would never see the kids again. My reasons for finding photos and for wanting a successful trial motivated me to action.

"Make a poster and send it all over the country," a friend urged me one day.

"What would I say," I asked nervously. It seemed like such a bold thing to do. I closed my eyes for a moment and could see a milk carton with my children's pictures on it.

"Get me a picture of each of your kids," my friend answered. Two hours later we had completed the poster. In big letters at the top of the page read: *"CAN YOU FIND THEIR PICTURES?— These children were sexually assaulted by their father and their grandfather for a period of three years. Stills and videos were taken."* With the help of several friends, I sent out posters to over six hundred law enforcement agencies around the country.

One outcome from this poster mailing was invitations from the Los Angeles Police Department's Child Exploitation Division and from the Las Vegas FBI. Each invited me to spend a day in their office as both these cities maintained a prolific reputation of being a hub for child pornographers.

And so in early January, I flew down to Los Angeles and found myself sitting in the office of the Child Exploitation Division of the L.A.P.D. on Wilshire Blvd. Made up of five men whose entire lives were devoted to the welfare of children, this department brought to justice those who exploit children.

After briefly discussing the case with them, they led me into a room where against one wall stood over twenty feet of gym lockers. "This," they explained, "is where we keep confiscated materials found during raids and arrests." As an officer opened each locker, the contents were revealed, and a burning stench seeped into my soul. I gasped as I beheld the huge volume of pornographic materials—one hundred percent child pornography.

"All of these lockers contain pictures of kids?" I asked stumbling over my words. They nodded slowly as my eyes widened with horror and disbelief.

"Yes ma'am, that's it. You won't need to look through all of it, just the ones dated from your children's abuse. Even still it will probably take you all day to get through those. There's a lot." Slowly, I sat down at a nearby table and waited quietly. Soon, an officer brought me a cup of hot coffee and the first stack of magazines.

Though I had sat and listened to my children's testimonies of detailed abuse, and though I could not get the pictures out of my head what those filthy men had done to them, nothing could have prepared me for what I was about to experience. In my wildest imagination, I could not have believed such things were done to children in this country on a wide scale; I could not have imagined child pornography is one of the most lucrative industries in America.

Uneasily, I placed the top magazine in front of me. I opened the first page and gazed upon a naked boy of about seven standing near a naked man. The lad had a young, innocent face but wore no smile. The man's face hid in shadows, while the boy performed a sex act on the man. Next page, more boys, more men, some boys as young as two, all engaged in some perverse sexual deed; picture after picture, page after page. On finishing the first magazine, heaves of nausea welled up within me. *I cannot go on looking*, I screamed silently. My head was hurting; I looked up, glanced around. No one was in sight. I wanted to cry aloud, to run, to find the iniquitous villains who did these things and kill them. My chest felt tight. My heart raced erratically. *There's no way I can sit all day looking at pictures like this. I can't do it! No way at all! Why did I even come here? Why?* I took deep breaths as I forced myself to remember why, why I came. It was for my kids, my babies. *This could help my kids. I must continue, must be strong. There is no time for weakness, not right now.*

I opened the next magazine. This one had mostly little girls, girls staging sexual acts with men or sometimes with each other. Magazines carried titles such as: Boy Lovers of America and Before Eight or It's Too Late (a club whose motto says children are sexually undesirable after eight years old), and so on. Some pictures were color photos, some black and white, all of them children. As I turned the hideous pages, after the initial shock (though it never goes away), after the initial pangs of nausea, I tried to focus merely on the kid's faces. I tried to block out the acts they were forced to do. When one of the officers passed by my table, I quickly shut the magazine in front of me and waited until he passed, thinking somehow I could protect him from seeing what he saw every day.

I saw few smiles on the faces of the little children, those under seven or eight. Sometimes looks of horror silently cried out from the pages, often looks of shameful humiliation. The older kids smiled at times, though none appeared to be smiles of genuine happiness, the kind of smile you have when life is truly wonderful. In many of their lives they had been doing this so long, they could never know what happiness is. The closest they might come to that is having a day when no one asks them to perform some sexual deed.

One girl's picture kept popping up in various magazines, different pictures of her but the same girl. Her name was Eva. Her voluptuous, blonde, curly hair hung softly over her bare shoulders and chest. She wore heavy eyeliner, ruby red lipstick complemented with lots of bright blush. Eva sat naked, hands folded in front of her, her legs crossed seductively. She could have easily passed for a woman posing for Playboy or Penthouse, or a woman of the streets standing on her corner, easily that is, except for one thing … Eva was five years old! Eva wore no smile on her young face, no light shining out of her eyes. What light she had been born with had faded long ago.

Minutes turned into hours; the day wore slowly on. One large ominous stack of magazines sat separately in the lockers. No need to look at those, I was told. My kids unquestionably weren't there. In this *special group* lie the pictures of murdered children, murdered during sex! Hearing this, I wanted to crawl in a hole and never face the world again. *What will I be like after today? How will I ever love, ever trust, ever live again?*

As I turned page after page, looking for a face that resembled my child's face, I discovered no child was immune. As I beheld blue-eyed children, brown-eyed children, green-eyed children and every possible tone of skin and hair, I realized the only real credential to be eligible is youth, usually before their bodies begin to mature.

Finally, my day with the L.A.P.D. ended. I had managed to sift through the debris of materials dated late enough to possibly be those of my children. Only once did I come across a picture resembling one of my kids. A little girl staring up at her perpetrator with big, frightened, brown eyes looked like my Rachael. Upon seeing it, I jumped up and dashed in to the officers' room. "I think I found a picture of my daughter." As we compared the picture with the one I had brought with me, all agreed it was a near identical comparison. However, when we turned the photo to its backside, the manufacturing date clearly read 1976, one year before Rachael was even born. It had somehow gotten mixed up in the wrong pile.

Bittersweet feelings of disappointment enveloped me. Though I fervently wanted to find pictures of my kids, the very thought of actually finding them, seeing them, scared me to death. But this one nearly-the-same photo was not Rachael's. It was not my daughter—just somebody else's.

Five o' clock came gratefully yet brutally. No pictures, no evidence, but at last I could walk away from this room, these lockers which only reminded me exactly how existent, how painfully existent my children's own locker of abuse was.

That night, as I glanced out of my hotel window at the city lights below me, I asked God that what I had experienced that day would not remain in my head forever. My heart, what was left of it, died that day, and only God could bring it back to life. As I prayed, I cried softly. I would never be the same again. Life had stolen first from my kids, and now it had stolen from me.

In the morning, I flew to Las Vegas to spend the day at the FBI headquarters. Roger Young instantly became one of my heroes. Not only was he a Christian man who loved the Lord dearly, but he battled the crimes committed against children and had done so for years, just as his father before him had also done.

He confirmed to me what I had already been told by other agents. A definite, predictable pattern often occurs with severely abused youngsters. From what was happening to my children, the girls especially had been nearing the time in their lives when the next step by the Crawford's could have included kidnapping and total submerging them into the world of pornography and prostitution. I thought about Tom's boss who was Tom's apparent first attempt to prostitute my daughters.

Flying home after my two-day *educational* trip, flying way above the clouds, I tried to envision a world without pain, without sin, without tears. What had we done to this home called Earth? What were we doing to these beings called children? And what ever could God be thinking as He gazed upon our sins? How could I ever smile again knowing and seeing what I had seen? It didn't seem possible that I would ever be happy again, ever look at life through eyes of joy.

By the time Christmas came, many in the community knew about the case. What could have been a very dismal Christmas, turned out to be one of the best the kids ever had. People from all over town, hearing about the lady whose four kids had been abused, brought gifts of toys, clothes and food to us by the armful. When Christmas Eve rolled around and a fellow from the Dream Tree brought yet another armful of gifts, I felt nearly embarrassed by all the giving. I then realized God intended it to be a special Christmas for my children as they embraced the love of so many.

That night, when the children finished hanging their stockings and hopped onto the couch to hear a bedtime story, we suddenly heard the sound of jingling bells outside our door. I alone expected this guest. "What's that sound?" I inquired with a look of surprise and a twinkle in my eyes. Why it sounds like bells, like ... Santa Claus." I leaped to my feet and headed for the door.

Turning around to catch a glimpse of their expressions, I saw they were no where in sight. Frightened, each one them had taken cover behind chairs and under tables, leaving little Emily on the couch alone, staring in bewilderment. Matthew peeked out from behind the couch, again holding a piece of firewood.

I opened the front door and in bounded Santa Claus (alias Officer Johnson with wife elf), jingling, and ho-hoeing all the way into the middle of our living room. "Aren't there any children here?" he cheerfully beckoned. Slowly, one by one, each came out of hiding, Matthew dropping his wood, smiles taking the place of worried little frowns. Within seconds, they gleefully crowded around Santa, stroking his snow-white beard, touching his coat with the jingle bells and of course, anxiously waiting to see what he would pull out of his big red bag. Tonight, there would be no gloom in this house. The sadness and hardship had been put aside while "visions of sugar plums danced in their heads."

Trial dates were set and trial dates were canceled as each side sought more time to prepare. The defense seemed desperate to obtain witnesses who could discredit me. Their strongest argument insisted I had made up this story and rehearsed it with the kids: It had to be the mom who invented such a tale. To say kids created such an intricate story, even *they* knew was too far fetched. Either *I* made it up, or it was true.

The FBI in Kansas maintained steady contact with us and were planning to arrest my ex-father-in-law. F.B.I. agents joined their local police who had already interviewed the kids by telephone. One day, the police from Tom's hometown called. They had obtained a search warrant and eight federal and local officers were going to the Crawford house. They assured me Ralph would be arrested by the end of the day. "Whether we find anything or not, our plan is to bring him in and charge him." It was clear they believed the kids.

The officers spent an entire shift at the house looking for pictures of the kids. But in spite of the nearly eight hours of searching, they found nothing other than some Playboy magazines and a roll of undeveloped film behind the master bedroom bed. The two month lapse of time from initial disclosure gave the Crawford's plenty of time to clean the place up. Even still, they took Ralph to the station upon which time he dictated a two page long statement. The paper, which I later read, was an exhaustive list of false accusations against me. Ralph stated I had been accusing men of sexually assaulting me or the kids for years, referring to my hitchhiking incident in Arkansas in 1973 and to a man I knew years earlier who had been caught molesting little girls (not mine) in a church community. Ralph did his best to paint me as a lunatic and a religious fanatic who went around accusing men of rape.

Shortly after this, Ken Thompson called me one day and said the Kansas police had been given a picture from Ralph. The photograph showed a woman sitting seductively on a bathroom toilet with only skimpy underwear on. Ralph told the police in Kansas the woman was me! The picture would arrive the following day. "I can tell you right now, Ken—that picture will not be me. This is some crazy notion of the Crawfords."

Thompson called up the following day. "I don't know what Ralph thinks he's up to, but this picture doesn't even resemble you."

"Didn't you believe me Ken?" He felt bad for having doubted. It hurt me deeply that such things were happening. *I* wasn't the one molesting kids. *I* hadn't broken the law, yet really, the way it stood, it was I who was on trial. The mother of the abused children was being torn up into little pieces, dissected, looked at through a microscope, and when nothing could be found to look at, someone was there to make things up.

Authorities in Kansas did not arrest Ralph Crawford. The FBI couldn't without photos, which they had hoped to obtain during the search. The police in Kansas grew progressively skeptical about the children's accusations and chose simply not to believe them but rather go with Ralph's version. I felt sure if they had met the kids and I face to face, they would have chosen differently. But with Ralph emitting his venomous deceptions unchallenged by anyone, he was able to portray any kind of picture he wanted. On top of that, Ralph was a very good friend of the mayor's and a prominent businessman in his community. At any rate, Ralph was not going to be charged—and not a thing could be done about it.

In the meantime, private investigators hired by the Crawford's attorney began an extensive investigation on me. Going door to door in my neighborhood they interviewed and interrogated. Were there men who slept at my home? Did I drink? What kind of parent was I, and so on? They hunted down people I had not seen in years tracing as much of my past as possible. In the end, after they had located countless friends and acquaintances all the way back to the early seventies, they were unable to find anyone who could back up Ralph's accusations.

The local police and the DA's office thought it only appropriate for me to take a polygraph test in light of Ralph having done so and passed. I agreed to cooperate and take the test myself. This wasn't a case between Tom and the kids anymore, I thought, but rather a battle between my ex-father-in-law and myself. With wires strapped to my arms and body, I answered yes or no to questions such as, "Did you tell your children to say they were molested?" and "Did you molest your children?" As they unstrapped the wires and belts and told me I had passed, I thought about victims of sexual crimes. Feeling like a victim myself now, I understood a little why so many didn't report. How does a hurting and frightened abused child or woman face such scrutiny? Surely, it would feel like being raped all over again. In a sense, that is how I felt.

With a trial in Oregon to prepare for, energies turned to the State of Oregon vs. Tom Crawford; I never gave up hope that evidence would be found in time to avoid such a trial. The roll of film which had been confiscated during the search in Kansas was developed. The Kansas police sent one *unusual* picture to Thompson. This picture depicted Matthew and Rachael, dressed in shorts and summer tops. They were posing on a lawn chair, laying together legs wrapped around each other and kissing in adult like fashion. Though this could not be considered pornographic because they wore clothing, it fell under the legal term *erotia*. When authorities asked each child separately who took the picture, they answered unanimously … their grandmother!

During these months of trial preparation, a high-charged energy emitted from the four kids. At times, they behaved like chickens with their heads cut off, running through a locked up barnyard, screeching, "Get me out of here."

One day, Rachael came running into the house. "Mama, Matthew fell out of the upstairs window!" Dropping my broom to the floor, I tore out to the yard and found Matthew lying on a bush under the second story window. As I picked him up, he whimpered softly.

"What happened," I cried out. Then, my eyes spotted a white sheet laying on the ground. Looking up against the exterior wall of the house I saw white sheets hanging from the window, several white sheets tied together in rope like fashion.

"We tried to slide down the house," Peter spoke up. Sarah, Rachael and I stared in astonishment. "I did it right Mommy," my youngest son boasted, "But Matthew forgot to hold onto the sheets." I was speechless. I wasn't quite sure what the boys were trying to do that day—*maybe trying to escape from the whole mess*, I thought. *Not a bad idea!*

The State dropped charges against Tom's old boss, saying the case was too weak. Ken said he wanted all our energies to go into the Crawford case. "These are not easy cases to win," he told me time and again. "Little children do not make the best witnesses."

Still, I couldn't understand why they didn't at least try to get this rapist, but I was given no say over this decision. My hate for this man only intensified. Because he was a stranger, I considered his abuse against Rachael and Sarah more of a violent assault. This stranger forced himself on two little girls—terrifying them, threatening them as if they were just some throwaway trash.

As January came to a morbidly cold close, a depressing helplessness engulfed me. My mother suggested I spend an hour with a psychiatrist she knew. Three days later I sat in the office of this understanding man, pouring out my heart to him. After I told him the whole story, he felt as depressed as I was and knew there was little he could say to help. But I thanked him and appreciated the opportunity. It was after five when I drove away from the doctor's office. Winter's early darkness was quickly descending.

Suddenly, it occurred to me that only three blocks away sat the work building of Tom's boss. All other thoughts vanished from my mind. The man who raped my daughters was walking around as a free man; oh how I hated him! An overpowering compulsion to see him ground its grip into my being. Slowly, I turned onto his street and spotted the old run down office. I pulled over to the curb and parked just a few hundred feet away. Then, only minutes later, out of the building he walked. I stared, then squinted my eyes and glared. *It's him*, I murmured to myself. Waves of rage flooded me, more than I realized had been inside. I couldn't seem to breathe. As he stepped towards the curb, I pulled out, rolling down my window as I sped by, and I screamed at him. I then slipped around the corner and headed for the freeway.

Shocked by my own outrage, perspiration beaded across my forehead. I slowed my speed then started to cry. Tears I had bottled up and been too afraid to release now had no barriers. I wept bitter unrestrained tears. Alone in the car was the only safe place I could truly allow myself to be so vulnerable, to express the horrible fears and anguish that would not go away. As I neared home, I dried my tears, straightened my hair then crawled back into the shell that would hold all those around me together.

Tom Crawford told me once he had an Uncle Steve who lived in California. He was considered the black sheep of the Crawford family. At the time Tom said this I gave it very little thought. But now I began putting two and two together. *If this man is the 'black' sheep of the family, then maybe he's opposite of them and is a good man.* An inner nudging told me to find him. At the library using California phone books, I collected every Steve Crawford or S. Crawford listed in that state. Soon, I had over twenty names.

The following day, while the children napped, I dialed the first number. "Hello, is this the home of Mr. Steven Crawford?" No Steve there, only a Stella. Down the list I went. Some numbers were disconnected, others were Stanleys or Samuels. By the 12th number, I realized what a long shot this was, and I felt silly for trying it in the first place. I dialed the next number then waited.

"Hello," a man's deep voice answered.

"Hello, I'm trying to reach Steven Crawford."

"This is he speaking. Who is this?"

"Are you the Steven Crawford related to Ralph Crawford in Kansas?"

"Yes, I am." Bingo! I introduced myself, told him I had been married to one of Ralph's sons. He was surprised to hear from anyone in the family, hadn't in years and wondered what he could do for me.

"Something awful has happened. Tom Crawford was arrested for molesting his children."

"I'm not surprised to hear that," he said.

"What do you mean?" I asked intently, a flash of shivers inching up my arms.

"Ralph is a very evil man; no doubt his son has followed his footsteps. But it's not entirely Ralph's fault. Our father, George Crawford, physically abused all of us. I was the oldest, and I got tired of the beatings, so I ran away at sixteen. I never went back. Most likely Ralph got the brunt of the abuse."

"Did your father molest any of his kids?"

"Not me, but I would suspect he did the girls. In 1922, he and my mother owned a mercantile in a small Iowa town. George was caught raping some of the local farmers' wives, and the men of the town forced him to sell his store and leave. He then moved the family to Kansas where he later was caught sexually abusing handicapped patients at a hospital he did janitorial work for.

Steven and I talked for over an hour. He spoke openly and candidly about his brother, Ralph. When I told him about all of the threats, he emphatically remarked, "Ralph is dangerous. He would think nothing of killing someone. You had better get yourself a gun." When I said good-bye to my children's great-uncle, I thanked him for his honesty. Though we would never talk to each other again, I was in debt to him for handing me the missing pieces of the puzzle.

The horrible sins of the fathers for the Crawfords hadn't been drinking after all. It was physical and sexual abuse. Tom had been a victim of it. Ralph too, had been a victim and maybe even George. My kids were the fourth generation to be affected by this sin. Now however, the sin that haunted this family for generations no longer maintained secrecy, and when that secrecy ended so did its power. The physical law had been destroyed by a higher law, the higher law that Christ died for, that He lived for.

A bittersweet sense of awe struck me—sweet, to see how great God's ever existing power was, bitter, to think of the damage that had already been done. Logic told me three years of abuse was short compared to generations and generations, but in my heart three years was like an eternity. I knew then no matter how much time elapsed, and no matter how well we went on with our lives, the pain and the scars of this would never completely go away, not for me, not for my children.

Discouragement and despair slowly wove their twisted arms around me the closer we got to the trial date. I had run out of people to call and letters to write. These things had helped me hold on to my sanity. "What is hope?" I questioned privately in my journal. "Faith, joy, peace, where have they all gone? Jesus, I still believe in You, but I am wondering what is going on. These past eleven years I've prayed, I've read Your word, I've worshipped, I've loved and forgiven. But now I stand empty handed. My children's youth and innocence have been robbed, my faith shaken and my heart, I think, has died. I've called people all over the country; there's no one else to call. I've sent posters to every possible place; there are no more places. I've written letters; there's no one left to write. I've watched my children suffer immensely since their days of disclosure. I've seen them cry and wake up in the middle of the night in horror from dreams too much for them to bear."

One week before the trial was to begin, we started mandatory evaluations with a Dr. Robert Jacobs, the psychologist chosen by Tom Crawford's attorney. The court mandated all four children and I must attend. Once again I refused to go and once again the court threatened me with contempt if I did not comply. *How hilarious to think I could end up in jail before Tom,* I laughed painfully to myself.

We spent three days with Dr. Jacobs. Nearly half of that time was conversation between Dr. Jacobs and I. After all, the defense would go to court saying this had been my diabolical plot to stop visitation. We also went through a series of psychological tests.

We finished with the interviews on Friday just before lunchtime. And then … a very strange thing happened. Fred Nicholas, Tom Crawford's attorney, supposedly had a reputation of being a morally upstanding gentleman. "Well if that's the case," I challenged once. "How can he defend a child molester?" I understood the process of the law—that everyone was entitled to fair representation—but how a good man could defend a person he *knew* brutally molested kids was beyond me. Even so, Nicholas continued through the many months to stand by Tom Crawford. However, on Friday afternoon, just hours after we finished our interviews with Dr. Jacobs, Fred Nicholas called Ken Thompson and announced he was withdrawing from the case. By law, he was not obliged to state his reasons, but after nine months he decided to back out. "Why Ken?" I asked later. "What would make him do that?"

"Though he did not say, there's only one obvious reason. Dr. Jacobs believed you and the kids and conveyed this to Fred Nicholas, convincing him that in truth he *was* defending a deviant child molester. Apparently he would not do this." A few years later, I discovered this to be exactly what happened.

With only a week to go before the trial and Tom now without a lawyer, another delay seemed highly likely. Much to everyone's surprise and relief though, my ex-husband quickly retained a new lawyer, Doug Hoffman, a lawyer who had in the past defended molesters and child murderers. The stage was now set for the most elaborate child abuse case our community had ever seen.

As the trial date drew nearer, I struggled to gain emotional and physical strength to go on. I searched for a place of solitude, of peace and happiness and found it only in my imagination. I daydreamed I was a maiden high up in a tower and saw in the distance a troubadour on his way to rescue me. His songs could be heard all across the land, and someday he would make it to the tower where the fair maiden waited.

Eight

And Justice For All?

"Behold, it is written before Me:
I will not keep silence, but will repay—
Even repay into their bosom—
Your iniquities and the
Iniquities of your fathers together,"
Says the Lord.
Who have … blasphemed Me on the hills;
Therefore I will measure their former work
Into their bosom."
Isaiah 65:6,7

Standing in the empty courtroom, we absorbed this unfamiliar territory. Tomorrow, the trial would begin. Hoping to shed some of the children's apprehension, Ken Thompson brought us to the very room where justice would be served—or denied. A large room, filled with stately looking oak chairs, benches and tables, it carried an aroma of permanent immovability and a demand for respect to all who walked through its doors. "This is where the judge sits," Ken said, pointing to the front area of the room.

"Can I sit on that chair?" Peter asked excitedly.

"Sure, just be careful. It's pretty high up." Peter squealed as he and Matthew raced to the judge's seat.

"Over there is where the jury sits."

"Whose side are *they* on?" Rachael questioned.

"Well, they are going to help the judge decide who's telling the truth; so tomorrow when you are talking, it's real important to just tell the truth. This is where you kids will sit," Ken continued, pointing to the stand.

"What about Tom; where will he be?" Sarah asked with sobriety. The boys stopped playing at the mention of their father's name. A stillness came over the room.

"Tom is going to be sitting over here." Ken stepped up to the counsel table which stood a few feet in front of the witness stand. The children would be face to face with the man who said he'd kill them or their mother if they ever talked. "And I will be sitting right there." The questions kept coming as the reality of things began to take form in the children's minds. As we left the empty courtroom, I turned to glance one last time and wondered if the American justice system would let us down.

It took the kids what seemed forever to fall asleep that night. Finally, the last one dozed off, and morning found its cumbersome way to our home. I ironed and put on my pastel lavender dress while the kids wore their best outfits, clothes really bought for Sunday

Court-Day Morning - Nervous But Ready

church not a court trial to testify against their father. With hair combed neatly in place, they seemed so small to be partaking in such a grown-up event. *How odd that children who have already been through so much abuse must now go through this. How very odd indeed!* My father picked us up, and we met Ken Thompson at his office. Soon we headed over to the courthouse across the street where reporters and other onlookers had already gathered.

During the trial, the State's witnesses would be given access to a private conference room in which we could wait for our individual turns to testify. The kids and I would stay all day while other witnesses would come and go as needed. I was not going to be allowed into the courtroom while each of the children testified. This was a law I never understood.

As the moment for the first witness grew closer, the conference room became increasingly quiet. I could almost hear the ticking of my father's watch; or was that the beating of my own heart? Someone poked his head into the conference room and said opening statements were finished. Minutes later the door opened again. The bailiff's voice came crisp and all too clear. "Catherine Crawford, you're the first witness." I rose to my feet, smiled at each of my children, then followed the officer down the corridor. My hands felt clammy; I hoped no one would notice my legs trembled. I walked with slow, steady steps, hoping to gain composure and increase confidence. This was the moment we had all been waiting for … the accusers facing the accused. Upon entering the courtroom, I was taken aback by all the people—the place was packed. Intentionally, I kept my eyes off my ex-husband.

Once sworn in, questions began with the State. Questions regarding background, history and disclosure were asked and answered. As Ken carefully and precisely covered the ground he intended to, I prayed the jury would see the truth.

The defense attorney, now had his turn, his turn to discredit me as a witness. Hoping to portray me as some kind of religious fanatic as Ralph had indicated, he asked, "Did you ever accuse Tom of being with the devil because he smokes and drinks?"

"No."

"Never said anything like that?"

"That he was with the devil?"

"Well, that this was the work of the devil?"

"I don't know. I know I haven't said that in the last six years to him. He and I have had conversations over the last few years during his visitations about his smoking pot and drinking in the presence of the children, and I was concerned about that."

"How about the smoking of cigarettes?"

"I haven't talked to Tom about cigarettes in the past six years." He went on and on about the cigarettes. I had nagged Tom about quitting when we were married. I couldn't believe they were making such a big issue out of it. I could only assume they hadn't found anything else to talk about.

"Did you have any thoughts or premonitions there would be any problems with child abuse?"

"When Tom first came back and said he wanted to start seeing the children, the thought did occur to me based on a couple things I knew from his past."

"Well, did you tell the children to watch out for Tom?"

"No, I never did. I had told the children at times ... on a couple of occasions I had said, 'Sometimes even daddies will touch in a wrong way.' But I never said, 'Your father will do this.'"

"Had you concerns about Tom's ability to take care of the children?"

"Well, yes."

"What was this relative to?"

"It was relative to his drinking. He drank in the morning, in the evening and in the afternoon. He drank quite a bit, and that did concern me.

At last, his cross-examination concluded. During the entire hour and a half on the stand, my right leg was crossed over my left whereupon my foot fell asleep. Stepping down from the platform, I had no feeling in that foot at all. Holding onto the edge of the rail thinking I might fall, I stepped into the middle of the room. As soon as my sleepy foot touched the floor, I started to go down and would have fallen completely if it had not been for Ken Thompson and a court-room assistant who came rushing to my side. Placing their arms under mine, they nearly carried me out. The following morning my ankle was swollen to twice its normal size, and I limped for a week.

The moment arrived when the State called Sarah to testify. Suddenly my courage vanished. Oh how I wished we could just walk away from that building. *How did I let this go so far, so far that now the kids will have to face Tom?* I hugged Sarah then stepped back as she walked out the room and down the hall. *This is like sending my daughter to the guillotine,* I now realized.

Ken Thompson asked her questions pertaining to the actual abuse. Sarah described how Tom had forced her to commit sexual acts with a dog. As she sat still as a mouse, her hands folded on her lap, she clearly explained what Tom said he would do to her mother if she ever told.

While Ken Thompson's questioning of Sarah came in gentle waves, Hoffman's was anything but. He shot lengthy, repetitive and intimidating questions, trying to confuse her by requesting precise dates and times, particular clothes worn on various occasions and asking misleading questions. Obvious to many in the room, his plan was to embarrass, humiliate and discredit any way he could. "How many times did you have sex with Tom?" he bluntly asked.

"I don't know."

"What would your estimate be?" he pressed, glowering into her eyes.

"A lot, but I don't…"

"Well, are you saying two times, five times, ten times?" he crisply pressed.

"More than twenty, I guess," she answered. Her lip quivered. Hoffman wasn't finished. How many times did such and such happen? How many times did this or that happen? If she couldn't give an amount, he pushed her until she came up with some number. They were *always* high numbers. He demanded to know why she had not disclosed as early as the other kids had. "I don't know," she answered.

"Well, why did you decide to talk to the policeman?"

"Because everybody else was, and my mom hadn't got hurt yet." The attorney then told Sarah she had been lying. She insisted she had not, and he shot back that she indeed had.

Sarah broke down into tears. The judge called a recess. By the time Sarah returned to the conference room, her crying had turned to heaving sobs. I could not handle seeing her in this state.

"That's it," I cried out, rising to my feet. "She's not going back in there! They are not going to do this anymore. We're through!" Ken Thompson took me by the arm and quickly ushered me out to the hallway as my father rushed to Sarah's side.

In Ken's always-kind voice, though a little sterner now, he looked intently at me, "Catherine, don't let the kids see you like this." I pulled my arm away and ran down the hallway. Suddenly, without warning, I was standing in a waiting room and there before me, sitting just a few feet away, sat the entire Crawford family. My entrance startled them. My mind raced erratically. *The child molesters—every one of them. Face to face, the real moment of truth.* Though some would always wonder who spoke the truth, everyone in that room knew, really knew the wickedly horrible truth ... My chest tightened. The room swirled in slow motion. I stared wildly at them as visions of my children's abuse ransacked across my mind—the rape, the sodomy, the pictures, the dog, the threats—yes the threats that kept my children silent. Hate that had been escalating for months swelled up, bursting out like a dam of water held back too long. *Only the innocent speak...* "You people ought to die," I screamed. A split second behind me, Ken Thompson pulled me by the arm to a room away from all others. I stood near him, my breathing intense, my arms crossed while I diverted my eyes away from his.

"Catherine, don't let the jurors hear you. Catherine, Catherine." His voice, repeating my name, came like a gentle breeze as he drew me back to reality from a flash of rage. *Is this what temporary insanity is? Is this how one tragedy leads to another?* As I took deep breaths and tried to regain composure, I asked God to show me the way, to give me the strength.

Day two came. One of the jurors called in sick, leaving only eleven jurors. Both sides agreed by verbal consent to continue, needing ten votes to concur a verdict. Legally this was allowed as long as the defendant signed a written consent. Somebody forgot to have Tom sign.

Hoffman continued testimony with Sarah. He persisted with the same course of questioning as the day before, the same questions over and over, rephrasing them differently in hopes of tricking her and catching a lie. It became so apparent that finally the judge spoke up. "Mr. Thompson," the judge began. "It has been asked and answered."

"Yes," Ken replied.

"The objection is sustained." It was a peculiar thing to happen, the judge making an objection—a reflection of Ken's less aggressive nature.

In the conference room, the bailiff informed us Sarah was finished, and Rachael would be next. At the mention of her name though, Rachael started crying as she recalled what transpired the day before with Sarah.

Matthew would have to go next. I wasn't sure Rachael would be able to testify. She was a fragile little girl and easily frightened. Six -year-old Matthew climbed to the stand looking carefully around him. Remembering Thompson's words to look straight at him, Matthew focused his gaze on the district attorney whom he had come to trust. In the course of thirty minutes, Matthew gave an account of his abusive years with Tom, telling how his dad said he would kill his mom if he ever told. "How did you feel about doing that stuff with your dad? Did it make you feel good or bad?" Ken asked.

"Bad."

"Did you want to do that stuff?"

"No."

On cross-examination, Hoffman tried to trick Matthew into saying I coached him, telling him what to say. "Have you discussed all these things with your mother?"

"Yes."

"Have you talked to her about what you should say?"

"Yes, I told her what I was going to say in court." Matthew was the one who finally broke secrecy. Tom Crawford's emotional bond with the boys had been much weaker than his with the girls. As I discovered after disclosure, he spanked the boys with his belt often, and at times, he seemed deliberately mean towards them. On one particular Christmas day, I brought the kids over to Tom's apartment. When we arrived, they all raced lickety-split into his living room to see their gifts. There, in the middle of the floor, sat three shiny new bicycles, a small red one for Peter and two larger girl's bikes but none for Matthew. Matthew raced to the bedroom, his eyes wide with hopeful anticipation. *Surely, his is in there,* I thought to myself as I watched the scene unfold. But instead of a shiny new bicycle waiting for him, laying on the floor in a hundred different pieces was an old rusty used bike.

The look on Matthew's face, the quiver on his lips, will stay implanted on my mind forever. He never cried, never said a word, yet another stab pierced the already torn heart of a little boy.

Surprisingly, Hoffman interrogated Matthew very little but long enough for the jurors to hear of the horrendous abuse Matthew had endured.

Peter, who had just turned five, was next. His eyes were wide with wonder as he sat himself down on the stand. He seemed less nervous than the others did, not being fully aware of the magnitude of the situation.

He answered every question with accuracy and truth. When it was Hoffman's turn, he went pretty easy on him. Even in *his* mind, he must have known that riding on a little kid like that could make him look like a heartless mongrel. Besides that, Peter's answers, though often in only nods and shakes, made a strong

Peter

statement, not of a child who made up stories but rather a child who was involved in an incestuous relationship with his father.

A second time Rachael was beckoned to the stand. "Do you think you can go in there honey?" I asked my little girl.

"I'll try Mommy." Doubts ran through my mind whether she could do it, but she amazed us all as she rose from her chair, gently laid her crayon down, then followed the bailiff down the long corridor and into the courtroom. With her big, brown eyes she peered around the room. Spotting her father, she wondered what he was thinking. Thompson asked Rachael to describe in detail the abuse that had occurred.

Hoffman took his turn, like a vulture going in for the kill (he hoped). Determined to confuse and intimidate, he focused on dates, times and places. He made a serious attempt to get her to say I had put her up to these stories and asked whether I had ever said anything about her dad concerning good and bad touches.

"No," she answered. When he began zeroing in on dates and times of various interviews, tears welled up in her eyes and dropped like splunkets of rain.

Hoffman hoped to lead Rachael into saying I had told them their dad was a bad person, before my knowledge of the abuse. "Before these things happened, did you ever have talks with your mother where she said Tom was a bad person?"

"No," she answered truthfully, for I never had.

"Was there ever anything you remember about smoking and being bad—people who smoke being bad people?"

"She said smoking is bad for Tom's lungs."

"Okay, nothing else?"

"No." Hoffman spent much of his time discussing Tom's cigarette smoking. Tom Crawford felt sure I had brainwashed the children over the years, convincing them he was a bad person because of his smoking. However, this was nothing more than an illusion in his mind, and his attorney was unable to prove anything otherwise. I now attributed these illusionary ideas of Tom's and his emotional immaturity to his own abused childhood. Outside of any sexual abuse that most likely took place when Tom was a boy, Ralph constantly belittled Tom with name-calling and other ridiculing, often calling Tom *stupid boy*. Tom confided in me once that for his thirteenth birthday his father took him to New York City. For his gift that year, Ralph hired a prostitute and presented her to his son. It was the night he lost his virginity.

Colleen Dursham, the State's main expert witness, now came to the stand. She described typical symptoms of exploited children which included fear, anxiety, eating and sleeping disturbances, breakdown in communication and breakdown in relationships with friends. She said that as each child has a different personality and different method of handling and coping, so too each reaction to abuse, each child's symptoms would vary one from another.

Colleen described Sarah as a very rational, intellectual child who always tried to keep her emotions under control. "She does not like to appear vulnerable, and her basic feeling of the situation was one of tremendous conflict. She had developed a very specific pattern of behavior, that is, she knew exactly what was expected of her, she knew she was supposed to lie quietly in her bed, she was supposed to keep her mouth shut, she was supposed to wait until things were done. She needed to be sure and check after her father left the bedroom to see where he was, because he did not like her to get out of bed and go to the bathroom afterwards. Colleen explained how Tom had been able to make her believe she was an adult and his lover, though only seven years old at the onset of abuse. Because the abuse had gone on for so long and happened so many times, Sarah had begun to accept the abuse as a given in her life.

Colleen then described Rachael as wavering between emotional extremes, one minute seeming like a little child and talking that way then the next minute sounding two or three years older than she really was. She described one of Rachael's most difficult situations as being that with the dog. When Rachael first described the dog incident to Colleen, Colleen said she seemed more concerned about the dog's discomfort than her own. Rather than "I feel bad," it was, "This dog is in pain."

Rachael recounted to Colleen nightmares in which people were shooting her mother, shooting her, or animals being ripped apart with people jumping out of them, holding shotguns.

Colleen said Matthew was the child most resistant to the abuse. "He was also the child who was most dramatic in terms of what he did physically in the playroom setting," she continued. "Matthew put on this show with three puppets. The first one would do what he called *tongue sucking* on the second puppet and would then imitate an intercourse movement with the two puppets. The second one, the one that was the victim supposedly, would do what Matthew said and scream for help, but what Matthew would do is open his mouth very wide and no sound came out, or it would be whispering, a very quiet sound that you could barely hear, and I would say, 'I can't hear the puppet screaming. If you're telling me the puppet is screaming, I can't hear that.' He said, 'That's because you're not none of the puppets.' I said, 'So you can hear them?' And he answered, 'I hear them screaming. I'm surprised it doesn't hurt your ears, it's so loud.'"

Colleen described Peter as a real physical, loud little boy. "He doesn't mind recounting incidents, but he doesn't necessarily see them as being all that important in his life. He's a lot more concerned about his siblings and his mother. He's probably the one that is most fearful of losing her, of her being hurt or his being taken away from her. He was willing to play with the puppets, ... but in every situation he would separate the family group, and then he would say, 'Okay here's Daddy; we're going to move him over here to the other side of the room; okay, now things are safe.'"

Later, I would read these stinging descriptions of my children, and my heart would break all over again as I absorbed the dramatic damage that had been done to my babies.

The defense called Ralph Crawford to the stand. Holding his head high, my ex-father-in-law always maintained a kind of military stance. He was a man who demanded respect and obedience, a powerful man driven to success. When Ralph spoke, everyone listened ... and moved. No one ever defied him. At home, things were done

Ralph's way, or things weren't done at all. No one—not his wife, not his sons or his daughter—no one went against Ralph. Maybe that's why he figured he could get away with all this—because no one would ever defy him, not even the children of Tom Crawford.

As did all of the men in the Crawford family who testified, Ralph admitted having Playboy magazines around the house. In fact, he brazenly stated he was a member of the Playboy Club; no big deal, he said. Ralph vehemently denied having ever molested his grandchildren.

Tom's mother, Hilda, made her way to the stand when her name was called. A stocky woman, though not nearly as tall as her husband, she had a round face with rosy cheeks. She had often reminded her children that Ralph deserved the family's utmost respect for all of his hard work. She talked to me more than once about her alcoholic father and the frequent beatings she and her mother received while she was growing up. Living under the authority of an abusive man was no strange matter for her. When asked if she had ever witnessed any inappropriate sexual activities with the children, she adamantly answered, "Never, never, never."

Much to everyone's surprise, Doug Hoffman called Tom Crawford to the stand. Tom had never been able to communicate well. He often grew nervous when talking around others, but became especially jittery when he lied. Tom had put on quite a bit of weight since 1980, but now at the trial, he was thin, gaunt and tired looking. His hair was greased down, cut short to his ears. Tom stood just over six feet tall—his eyes no longer big, brown, kind, but rather squinty and unfocused.

During cross-examination, when Ken Thompson asked Tom what the two boys and he did that last night together, he nervously responded, "Well, one thing I recall, you know, vividly is, you know, we had a pizza, because I ordered a pizza, and we ate it. It was delivered, you know; I didn't go get it. And we just did our usual thing, sat around watching T.V. and nothing really interesting." Of course, he never mentioned having touched Matthew that night—never mentioned being afraid I might see the redness that his touching left on his son.

When asked why he initially agreed to give up his visitation rights after Matthew had first disclosed, he answered, "I had just been thrown in jail, and I just couldn't believe I was there and being accused of such an action, and I thought, my God, what is she doing to me? Why? Why? Why? And I thought the best thing for me to do is to get away from her. I mean, I didn't know what more she was up to. I thought if I could get away for awhile—I didn't know what was going on. I couldn't believe that I was being accused of this. I thought it was in my best interest to possibly not see the kids for awhile until I figured out what she was doing with me."

"Did you have some concerns about what Catherine was doing?"

"Oh man, here I am sitting in jail, a father of four children, and she's got my son saying that I've sexually molested him. I mean what do I do? She's crazy. She went crazy."

The final day of the trial finally arrived. Nearly thirty witnesses had testified. All I could think about now was Tom getting convicted. I hated him so, hated his family. A conviction would assure me Tom would never see the kids again. This I had been promised over and over again. It was the motivating factor for pressing through with the trial in the first place. I wasn't sure what would happen if the jury found Tom "not guilty." But I would *never* let the kids down again. I'd never let him touch them again.

After lunch, Ken Thompson rushed into the conference room to let me know I'd be going on the stand one last time. The courtroom was bustling when I walked in and took the stand. Jurors were getting settled; people talked quietly among themselves while attorneys gathered papers and prepared for closing statements.

Until this point, I had not even looked at my ex-husband. I had intentionally avoided him. However, while everyone in the courtroom was preoccupied, I lowered my eyes and glanced down on this man. What happened to me in that next moment, in the flash of an eye, no one there knew anything about, but it changed my life in a dramatic way..

The hate I felt towards Tom had become so strong, it resembled a growing, festering monster. Now, as I took this quick glance at him, a voice inside me spoke, that tiny still, small voice I knew to be the voice of God. Though no one else in the room heard the words, they were clear, precise, and cut like a knife. "It's true," the Lord said, "That if this man does not repent, he will spend eternity in Hell, but I want you to know, My heart is broken for him; My heart is broken that he is lost. I love him."

Like an earthquake that detrimentally shakes and disturbs the foundations of century old buildings, I too was shaken by these words. I knew they were not my own. For a brief moment—a split second in time—God opened my spiritual eyes, opened the window of *His* heart and gave me a glimpse of how God saw this sinful man, of how God saw all of mankind. And right there, the hate that had planted itself so deeply in my heart began to break. The Lord *would* commute His judgment, but His Heart was broken, for He loved all of mankind and wished none should perish.

No one in the courtroom that day knew what had taken place save the angels of God who stood in the empty corners. Though I never wanted to see Tom again, though I would never allow him to see or touch my children again, though I still wanted him convicted and sent to jail, I knew I would never again hate him as I had. I would see him for what he really was—a victim once himself. And even Ralph too had been a victim and perhaps his father before that, and God only knew how many generations there had been in this family who had been abused by the generation before. And through prayer and God's faithfulness, I knew the abuse was not going to be carried onto another generation. And now, after this shattering revelation of God's love for Tom and for all people, I was not going to have to instill in my children a hate and rage towards their perpetrators that too could destroy their lives. When I finished testifying, I returned to the conference room. With the children no longer there, I broke into a soft cry as I sat down. Kathy, a supporter, hugged me. Still moved by this touch from God, I whispered to her, "I feel so sorry for him." Kathy looked incredulously at me. It was the only time I ever cried for Tom Crawford, but I never forgot what God did that day to my heart.

Closing arguments began. Everyone, myself included, piled

into the courtroom. Sitting in the back row, now from the position of onlooker rather than partaker, helped me envision how my children must have felt when they testified. I tried to picture their little faces peering over the edge of the stand, gazing at so many people, telling things one does little more than whisper in a public arena.

Ken Thompson gave the jury that final picture on behalf of the children. Doing a kind of Clark Kent—Superman transformation, he stood before the jury, no longer sounding like a gentle, mild-mannered fellow but rather like one who speaks with commanding authority—one who speaks with dominating conviction that what he says, he believes. I saw clearly then his deep love for justice and his unwavering efforts to uphold it.

"The defense says," he began, looking directly into the eyes of the jury members, "that Catherine Crawford put the kids up to telling a story … I think it's clear that in order to get the types of incidents, the detail, the extent, the magnitude of what you've heard … it would be pretty clear that the kids couldn't have made this up on their own. I don't think anyone could possibly conceive the kids would have dreamed all of this stuff up by themselves. So the question is, did Catherine put the kids up to this fantastic story that never occurred? What is the motivation? Why did she do this? If she deliberately put these kids up to bizarreties that couldn't have occurred, why would she have the kids come up with such elaborate stories, such detailed stories? Why throw in so many people? Why have the act complained of so bizarre? Why not keep just Dad involved? Dad's the only problem, if it's visitation you want to cut off. You don't need to involve the whole family. You don't need to involve the ex-husband's old boss that the family doesn't even know."

Later, in the defense attorney's closing arguments, he said maybe I, the mother, actually believed the whole story, but hysteria set in, and now I was running with it and rehearsing with the kids things to say, adding more and more all the time.

He suggested I was a woman on a crusade, mailing out hundreds of posters, and I had lost touch with reality. All of these things I did, he said, were the actions of a mother gone lunatic.

Hoffman said what my kids testified to were nothing but blatant lies filled with inconsistencies. When Hoffman began calling my children names, I stood up and left the courtroom. A friend followed me, and we took a stroll outside under the trees, which were just showing their spring blossoms. Gulping in deep breaths of the fragrance, I sought strength for the coming moments.

When we returned to the courtroom, closing arguments were over. Someone said they saw the whole Crawford clan sitting around laughing, and what was that they overheard Hoffman saying to them? "…absolutely nothing to worry about." I feared it may be true. Few cases were won with merely young children's testimonies.

No one expected an early verdict, so when the court officer came to our room less than seventy minutes later, we were astonished. Quickly, we returned to our seats and waited. An eery silence filled the courtroom as I studied the faces of each of the jurors. Their looks gave no indication of what they had decided.

"Have you reached a verdict?" The judge queried the jury.

"Yes, your honor." The jury foreman handed a piece of paper to the bailiff who, in turn, passed it into the hands of the judge. He cleared his voice, eyed the courtroom for a brief moment then read, "We, the jury, find the Defendant guilty as charged." Muffled gasps filled the courtroom. The judge hit his gavel and demanded order. Even at that moment of victory, I was ordered to keep all my emotions contained. No shouts of joy, no verbal prayers of thanks, but Tom Crawford was guilty, and it had been proven in a court of law. All I could think about now was getting home to my children and holding them.

Nine

On The Run

Justice left awhile ago,
When *Little House on the Prairie* died.
Now I wonder what I'll do,
To keep my babies safe.
I want to take them,
Run and hide,
But there's just no place to go,
So I'll put them gently in the care
Of their Heavenly Father above.

Quickly, in hushed movements, I awoke my five children. "Why are we up when it's still dark, Mommy?" asked five -year-old Peter.

"Remember? We are going on a trip," I whispered.

"Oh yah," he mumbled.

Rubbing their eyes, stretching and yawning (suddenly remembering what day this was), the children put on their neatly laid out clothes. My baby daughter whined softly for her bottle. I changed her diaper and glanced towards the silver alarm clock— it was nearly four AM.

As Emily fidgeted and squirmed, I pulled a light, cotton dress over her head of wispy, blonde hair then topped it with a sweatshirt. It was cool outside now, but by noon, temperatures would soar into the nineties as we traveled through the desert regions of Eastern Oregon and Idaho in our Rambler station wagon.

Quietly, we shuffled into my parents' kitchen, taking in the aroma of freshly brewed coffee and lightly toasted bread. I peeked out the window towards our car and saw what resembled a modern day version of a covered wagon—the children and I the pioneers, heading into unknown frontiers. The lemon-colored car was packed to the roof with blankets, pillows, dishes and toys, leaving just enough room for five kids and a mom. Two metal racks sat fastened along the top of the roof, each overflowing with everything conceivable for survival. Household furnishings too big to take had been sold, never to be seen again. We could have pulled a trailer, but upon reaching the Canadian border the added luggage would make our story of a two-week camping trip that much more preposterous. That was what I would say though, a camping trip, two weeks at the most. Yet our intention was anything but. On the contrary, we were fleeing the home and the country we loved.

I clung to a desperate hope that Canada could protect my children from the horrible evil that chased us. "You'll never have to worry about him again if we win this case," authorities had promised me. Evasively, those promises slipped out of our reach, leaving the burden of protecting my children on my shoulders alone.

Three months earlier, on the very day the trial ended, the State of Oregon dropped eight remaining charges against Tom Crawford, which would have entailed three more trials. Ken Thompson said the children could not go through the trial trauma three more times. On that same day, after the jurors, reporters and spectators had gone, the judge released Tom Crawford on his own recognizance. "An upstanding citizen," the attorney insisted to the judge as he stood in the nearly empty courtroom. Tom returned to Kansas to await sentencing, which would take place later in the year.

Shortly after the trial, contrary to what I had been told before, I learned Tom would probably serve less than two years for his felony offenses. Upon hearing this, I sought the counsel of a local attorney who told me according to Oregon law, once a person had paid their debt to society by serving time in prison, they could no longer be punished for their crimes. Tom Crawford, I was told, would most likely receive visitation rights again, if he so desired.

Summer arrived, and I could not escape the heavy depression that enveloped itself around me. I tried hiding it from the kids but found our surroundings unbearable. Our house, our street, our town—everything was a constant reminder of what had happened. And suddenly it seemed as if no one was there to help us. We had been surrounded by friends, family, police and counselors for ten long months. Now, we were alone. For the State of Oregon, results had been tremendous. For others who knew us, a sense of victory was in the air. But for me, for my children, we were left alone to pick up the broken pieces of our lives. The emotional pain I had bottled up for so long was bursting to get out. Yet, I continued to keep a lid on what I feared was pain too great to face.

The children seemed fine, though I didn't see how they could be. *Perhaps we can just go on with our lives as if nothing has happened,* I thought to myself. The kids begged me not to make them talk about the abuse anymore. For ten months they had been court ordered from one evaluation to the next. I understood their request. *Maybe this is best—just forget all the evil and try to make our future something wonderful. One thing for sure, Tom Crawford will never get near my children again.*

For weeks following the trial, I combed newspapers, court cases and magazines. I discovered that far too many times, courts quickly restored visitation rights to fathers who had been accused of molestation. Many women, I discovered, gave in. However, some took extreme measures to protect their children. One woman actually put her daughter in hiding with relatives. She was arrested and put in jail when she refused to tell authorities where her daughter was. She sat in prison for eighteen months until finally President Bush Sr. pardoned her. I also learned about an underground movement that was taking place all across the country. An entire operation hid mothers and the children who were in danger of further abuse because of lenient court systems. These women, who risked all to protect their children, became my heroes. Anything less I saw as sheer cowardliness.

"I can't stay in this country any longer," I said to my mother and father. We sat alone in their living room, talking in hushed tones as the children played in a nearby room. "If I had done something four years ago, when I could not get protection for the kids, none of this would have ever happened. I'm not going to let it happen again. He will never sit in the same room as these kids again." Before my father was ready to consent to my outrageous idea, he insisted we seek the counsel of another attorney.

"That's right, Miss Crawford," the young lawyer said. "According to Oregon law, your ex-husband has a very good chance of obtaining visitation with his kids once he has served his time." Stunned and saddened, my father and I walked away in silence.

"I guess you have no choice, Catherine. You will have to go."

And so on July 5th, before the dawn of a new morning enveloped the silent darkness of our town, before the summer sun peaked over the horizon and the safety of night would vanish, we kissed my parents good-bye and drove away. They were the only ones in the whole world who knew where we were going. We waved until we could no longer see their pretty little house on a tree-lined street. I grasped the memory and never wanted to let it go. The children saw this as a great adventure and seemed eager. Perhaps they saw this as a way to forget the past. I too longed for that.

Three days later, we reached the Alberta/Montana border. As we sat in a line of cars, slowly inching towards the border patroller, my heart beat fast and the palms of my hands became clammy. "Okay kids, let Mommy do the talking. You can say hello and smile, but that's it."

"Okay Mommy," the kids chorused in unison. As our turn came, I reached for an envelope that contained our birth certificates and my green card. Being born in Canada and still being a citizen was certainly going to make this a lot easier, I hoped.

"Hello ma'am. Where are you heading?" the officer queried.

"We're going camping for two weeks then will probably visit relatives before heading home," I answered as I handed him our documents. He glanced back towards the children then carefully eyed the racks on top of the car.

"This is quite a bit of stuff you have for two weeks of camping."

"Well, with five children, it takes quite a bit," I answered politely.

"Yes, I guess so. Well, you have a nice trip now, and welcome back to Canada." As we drove on through the border, silence that demanded some answers filled the car.

"Okay, kids, you can talk now."

"Mom, did you lie?" asked seven-year-old Matthew.

"Yes, I did honey, a little bit. It's wrong to lie and I'm sorry. But I told you how important it is that we don't tell anyone we are moving here. Someday you will understand better."

"I understand now," he answered. *Yes, I suppose you do,* I thought to myself. *Perhaps you all understand a lot more than I realize.*

A few hours later we pulled into a small prairie town and found a modest looking but clean motel. "Is there a T.V. Mom? asked one of the girls.

"Yah, can we watch some cartoons?" followed Peter.

"No bad ones, Mom," Matthew assured me. I smiled at my children's sweet tender hearts. Those had not been robbed from them.

I no sooner got the key into the motel room door when they all leaped on the beds and turned on the television. Quietly, I laid down and closed my eyes.

After the children finally fell asleep, I listened to a summer thunderstorm's pelts hit against the window. "Oh, God," I prayed. "Please show us where to go. I'm not even sure we are doing the right thing, but I'm trusting you to lead the way."

The following day we continued driving north. Occasionally I stopped and studied a map. We drove on a highway called the Grizzly Bear Trail. If I kept going, it would take us right up to the Peace River—the place I was heading many years earlier when I had graduated from high school and hitchhiked in Canada. A lifetime had passed since then. Now I had five children, and we were on the run.

As the rain finally broke late in the afternoon, we drove into a small town in the middle of nowhere. *It will be hard to find us up here,* I thought to myself. "How's this place look, kids? Do you think you would like to go to school here?"

"Yah Mom," they sang in unison. Little Emily, now almost two, clapped her hands.

"This place looks really good," five-year-old Peter added. As we all peered out the windows, we saw more trees than houses. But there was a school, a store, a post office and a couple of churches. What more could we ask for? It seemed that all the members of the board unanimously agreed—if we could find a place to live before the end of the day, this would become home.

Within an hour and a half, we located a furnished duplex for rent, talked to the landlady and paid the rent. By dinner time, we were in our new place. While the girls made up the beds with fresh sheets and blankets I had packed, I cooked our first meal. Later that night, when the kids were all asleep, I began fishing through boxes looking for one particular item. There it was, wrapped carefully in newspaper and linens—Home Is Where The Heart Is. As I hung our embroidered picture on an empty white wall in the living room, I smiled as I thought of the children's expressions when they would see the picture hanging in the morning. "Remember," I will say. "We are always at home, as long as we're together."

Later that week, I went to see an attorney. It was risky, and I was counting on him believing me. He did, and within one week, the children and I had a new last name. Now, he said, I was safe to apply for a Canadian social security card, obtain employment, and we would even be able to receive Canadian social medical coverage, which all citizens enjoyed.

Just days earlier we had been Americans. Now we had new identities and were thousands of miles from anyone who could hurt us. I was determined to put Tom Crawford in the past and to give my children the best possible upbringing I could, even if it was so far away from the family and friends we loved so dearly.

One day, not too long after we had arrived, I drove the children to a beautiful, secluded lake ten miles out of town. In the distance, we saw the Rocky Mountains and were in awe of Canada's unpolluted beauty. On the way home from our picnic, we spotted a mother bear crossing the road with three cubs. It was an awesome sight. Though my heart constantly ached, the children and I had found some joy again in the simple things of life.

Just before school started, I began my search for a job. A neighbor told me about a road construction crew that might be looking for a flagger. I had never done such a thing but thought it was worth a try. I loaded the kids in the car and headed to the woods on an old forestry road. Several miles out of town, I found the construction sight. One of the men directed me to the foreman. Slowly, I drove towards him, stopping a few feet from where he stood.

"Are you hiring any flaggers?" I called out.

"No, we don't need 'em way up here." He looked astonished to see a young woman with a carload of kids. "Have you ever driven a packer before? We need a packer operator." He pointed to a huge, yellow tractor. My eyes widened in disbelief. *Is he asking me if I can drive that thing?* I gulped hard then answered,

"No, I've never driven one of those … but I can learn. I'm a fast learner and a hard worker. I really need a job."

"I haven't hired a woman in 28 years. But if you want the job, I'll give you a try. Be here at six tomorrow morning." As we drove away, the kids were bouncing with questions.

"Are you going to drive that big tractor, Mom?"

"How much are they gonna' pay ya' Mom?" I shuddered to think I was actually going to climb this monstrous looking piece of equipment. But the money was good, and we sure needed that.

My parents called and said Tom Crawford had been sentenced to nine months in jail! I was flabbergasted at the leniency the court had shown him. The Crawfords' had now hired a top-notch big city attorney who filed an appeal immediately after sentencing. The court allowed Tom to remain free until an appeal action was either denied or granted.

Signs of fall descended upon us even before summer officially ended. The children started school, and I began working with the road construction crew. The men in the crew were hard, toughened guys. They swore a lot, drank a lot after work and lived most of their lives away from their families. At first, I was very intimidated by their brusqueness and worldliness, but as time passed, I found them to be kind and often considerate towards me. Whereas at first they tried to impress me with their foul language, they soon made efforts to minimize their swearing when I was around. My nickname became *Born Again*.

The children adapted well to their new environment. They made friends and danced for joy when we had snow in October. My work hours were very long as the crew raced to finish the road before winter set in. I hired a neighbor woman to help watch the younger children while Rachael and Sarah learned to cook and clean. They were eleven and nine. I wondered if our knight in shining armor was ever going to arrive.

People in the small town were curious about us. Some asked just enough questions to leave me nervous about their intentions. I had told no one we were in hiding, but I knew they wondered what a woman with five kids was doing in the middle of nowhere so far from home. I began to suspect one might eventually turn us in. One particular woman and her husband began drilling the kids when I wasn't around. I did not like putting the kids in the position of having to cover up the truth. Perhaps if I had told these curious folks the whole story, they would have been sympathetic. But I had lost my trust in people, fearing we could be hurt at anytime.

Alberta, Canada— not too many miles from where we lived.

I began making plans to cover our trail. One day I removed the license plates from the Rambler and sold the car to a transient family. Thomas, a fellow from work who had befriended us, found a good cheap car and bought it for us. It was a very kind thing for Thomas to do, and I have never forgotten this act of goodness towards us. When the job ended in November, I grew increasingly concerned over nosy neighbors. Late one night I packed up the car, and we left the little town in Alberta. I feared this would become our lives—moving and constantly worrying about suspicious people. And yet, I was terrified of returning to the States, only to have a court restore Tom's visitation.

As we drove late into that night, heading east to Saskatchewan, a snow blizzard descended upon us. Not being able to see more than a few feet in front of me, I began crying. *God, what am I to do? All I have ever wanted to do is just raise my children and walk with You. But it is all such a struggle. I don't even know where we are supposed to go.*

Two days later we arrived in the city of Saskatoon. I had decided we were too conspicuous in a small town. *Here,* I thought, *we can blend in.* And so, we started all over. We found an inexpensive but clean house to rent; and I enrolled the children in a new school. I put an ad in the local paper advertising as a housekeeper. Within days, I landed several housecleaning jobs. I was thirty-two years old, but in spite of my nearly two years in college, I was unskilled. Changing diapers and housecleaning were my fields of expertise.

Right away we found a good church to attend. Though the people in this church seemed curious, they never asked questions. Somehow, I think we had it written all over our faces that we were in trouble and in great need of friends. They embraced us as if we were so. We found Canadians, in general, to be extremely hospitable people.

By Christmastime, temperatures neared twenty degrees below zero as neighbors made exclamations about such a warm winter! As I traveled across town to my various cleaning jobs, I shivered with a chill that would not leave my bones. Each night I soaked in a hot tub of water but could tell my strength and health were slowly being zapped. I began to lose weight and soon started to experience terrible pains in my back and groin area. The pain continued to worsen.

After weeks of agonizing pain and a steady deterioration in my health, I finally went to the doctor. "Well, Catherine, I think we better run some tests," he said. The test results came back inconclusive, and at first he thought I had a femoral hernia. He scheduled surgery, but then just days before the surgery, he decided the hernia did not exist.

During the next three months, twelve doctors examined me. My confidence in the doctors soon eroded as I was emotionally bounced from minor diagnoses to life-threatening ones. One team of doctors thought I might have bone cancer. And yet they were puzzled at the constant negative test results. Finally, one of the specialists suggested my health problems may be psychological.

I knew my pain was real, and coupled with the weight loss and fatigue, I began to believe I was dying. *Perhaps I do have bone cancer,* I told myself. *If I die here in Canada, what will become of the children?*

One evening, I sat down with the kids. "We need to have a family meeting," I said looking carefully at each one of them. "Mommy is sick, and I think we have to go back to Oregon."

"That's okay, Mom. God will take care of us," Sarah said most matter-of-factly.

"Yah, Mom," Rachael agreed. "God will protect us." I was once again amazed at these little people called my children. Nearly one year after we left Oregon, we packed up once more and this time headed home. I was afraid, but the kids were delighted.

To my utter surprise and relief, my doctor back home told me I did not have bone cancer. He did, however, find cancer in my bladder—extremely unusual, he said, for a young woman. The doctor scheduled surgery immediately. Two days later he removed a malignant tumor. We rejoiced when the prognosis was so encouraging though. I would not have to have any chemotherapy or radiation. "We'll check you every few months," Dr. Robinson said, "and make sure the cancer doesn't return." And to this day, it never has.

After the surgery, the pain in my back and groin continued to worsen. It became apparent this pain had nothing to do with the bladder cancer. And yet it was this pain that caused the tumor to be found. In essence, this mystery pain had saved my life.

Finally, my doctor sent me to a specialist who discovered I had a severe pinched nerve. He treated the problem and soon the pain disappeared. God had used this pinched nerve to bring us home. Wherein I believed I was coming home to die, I rejoiced to be alive.

Tom Crawford was in his second year of trying to get an appeal. For the time being, we were safe. He would leave us alone until he either won an appeal or served his time in jail. If it looked like he was going to gain access to the kids after one of those occurrences, I was ready to head back to Canada. But for now, we were home, and the children seemed happy.

Ten

On the Wings of a Dove

Oh that I had wings like a dove!
I would fly away and be at rest.

As weeks turned into months, I heard nothing about Tom Crawford. I knew he was hoping to win an appeal, but one appeals court after the next denied him. I tried not to think about it and was too busy anyway. Though outwardly I walked through the motions of life, I continued to feel dejected and hopeless. I just could not see beyond the pain. And my mind kept playing over and over this statement like a broken record, "No matter how hard you try, no matter how much you trust God, bad things keep happening. You can't even protect your kids."

October arrived and with it, the windy breezes of Autumn that chase away summer's muggy air. One night, after a day in which everything had gone wrong, I lay in bed crying out to God. I felt desperate to hear from Him and decided I would not go to sleep that night until I did. I cried my eyes out and spent what seemed like hours beseeching Him. I felt much like I did that night many years ago in Kansas when I stayed on my knees and gave my life to Jesus. Now, I felt that same anguish. *God, I have got to know you are with me. Somehow, please touch my heart.* I reminded the

Lord about the story of Jacob and how he wrestled with God until he received a blessing. *Lord*, I said, *I am not going to sleep until You give me a blessing, until I know you are here!* Eventually though I fell asleep. I had not even been able to stay awake to receive the blessing.

Early the next morning, I woke to noises outside my window. With my eyes still shut, I listened carefully. It sounded like a bird. Leaning over the bedstead, I lifted the curtain and beheld a beautiful robin dancing right outside my window. His beautiful red wings fluttered as he hopped around. He was so close I could have reached out and touched him.

And then, the blessing came. God was speaking to my heart: *Fear not my dear child, for I am with you, and I want you to be free. The birds of the air are free, and I created you to be free too. This little bird does not worry, nor does he toil. But he trusts in his Creator. You too can do the same. And no matter what happens, I will always be there.*

I felt flooded all over, like when I became born again. The pain lifted, the despair vanished. God washed me and touched me. I knew He had. For the first time since I discovered my children had been abused, I felt alive and joyous.

After spending a few more moments relishing in this beautiful morning rendezvous with God, I leapt out of bed and rushed down the hallway. I heard Saturday morning cartoons coming from the living room. "Come on kids," I called out. "We're going to the coast today." They danced around in jubilation, more so I think in seeing

their mommy so full of life and joy. We piled coats and hats, hotdogs and marshmallows and a pretty little kite into the car, and off we went. For two days we played and giggled and rested in God's peace.

As I sat on the warm sand, watching the waves fold up over the shore, I felt tremendous gratitude to the Lord. My children, I still had my children. They could have been kidnapped or murdered or just continued being secretly abused, but they weren't. They were with me, and we were still a family. We would always be a family. That was something that had not been taken from us—God truly had been gracious to us.

One day, nearly three years after I had discovered my children's abuse, the phone rang. "Catherine, this is Ken Thompson. I have some rather bad news." My heart sank as I listened. "Tom lost every appeals court he went to, and they tried every angle to win an appeal. Last week, the Oregon Supreme Appeals Court granted him one."

"On what grounds," I whispered, not able to speak words with any strength.

"On a courtroom technicality. If you remember, on the second day of the trial, one juror did not show up. Both sides agreed to this, but Tom was supposed to sign a statement. He never did. They won the appeal on the argument that his constitutional rights were violated."

"What does this mean?" I asked, holding back tears I would not allow to fall.

"It means we will have to go back to court if you and the kids are willing." As Ken spoke the words, and as I listened to this incredible situation, I knew I would not take the kids back to court. It had been so long, and they had not even once talked about the abuse in over two years. They had asked me to promise not to make them talk about it anymore, and I had agreed. No, I would not make them go back. But at that moment, I knew I was going to have to call the Crawford's bluff. And I knew Ken would never go along with it. As a district attorney he was not in a position to compromise his principles. As a mother, I was not in a position to compromise my children.

"Well Ken, then tell them that is what we are going to do. Tell them we are going to press charges again, and we are going back to court."

"Okay Catherine. I'm leaving this up to you." We hung up, and I leaned against the kitchen wall. I felt numb and unsteady. I looked out the window and saw my beloved children running and playing. Could we actually go into hiding again? What would that do to the children now that they were older and so established in the community? Tom had won an appeal which meant he would be acquitted—all because he did not sign a piece of paper. Was he going to come after the kids now? According to the law, he would be considered innocent unless found guilty again.

The following day Ken called again. "I have talked to Tom's attorney, and he has spoken to the Crawfords. They want to make a deal. If you will agree to not press charges again, Tom will allow his parental rights to be revoked, irreversibly."

"I want to see it in writing, in a legal document before I make any comment," I said to Ken.

The Crawfords wasted no time. Two days later their attorney delivered a document to Ken Thompson stating that Tom Crawford irrevocably relinquishes all his parental rights to the children once and forever. It can never be undone. At the bottom of the document lay Tom's signature. I in return would never file charges against him and would seek no child support. My children would no longer have a legal father but would no longer be threatened by the Crawford family.

The following day as I sat in Ken Thompson's office, I studied the paper carefully. I knew I wasn't going back to court—all I cared about now was having the assurance my children would be safe, that they could grow up without the threat of the Crawford family hanging over their heads. As for Tom's punishment and judgment, … that would be up to God now. Earthly courts had decided not to render justice. For Tom, he would have been better off to confess his sins and pay the price. What a terrible day judgement day is for the unrepentant heart!

As I sorted out these thoughts into different folders in my mind, I signed the paper. With the stroke of a pen, I bought my children's protection. It was all I had ever cared about, all I ever wanted for them. Now I could give them what every child deserves—rest and safety from the windy storm and tempest. We would take wings like a dove and fly away and be at rest … My children dance and giggle and play. Life whispers to them—*Let's go.* Laughter calls me to its side … Now, I really do know why.

Epilogue

Many years have passed now, and my babies have grown to young adults. Each of them has had to deal with their abuse in different ways—it wasn't always easy, and I wasn't always sure they were going to make it. But as they grew and matured they have all loved the Lord Jesus. The damage and pain caused by the Crawfords will always be a part of my life, a part of their lives. But we have come to see that God's love and mercy can override any pain, any damage that the enemy has caused. Without the Lord, I don't know how our lives would have turned out. I cannot even imagine. But He *was* there just as He had promised.

Let me tell you how my children are doing:

Sarah is a beautiful sensitive woman, married to a dear young man. They have a son (and a new baby on the way) who loves his parents so much, loves to play sports with his dad and tells Granna he wants Jesus to live in his heart. Sarah is so full of wisdom and so beyond her years. She is a nurse now, and she and her husband are foster parents to children in need. I have noticed something about Sarah— she always seems to be reaching out to the hurting of this world.

Rachael has grown into a tall, lovely young woman. She is exuberant and loving, and has a beautiful little daughter. Rachael is the one who makes sure she and her siblings get together regularly, and if there are ever any squabbles, she takes it upon herself to see to it that everyone makes up and forgives. Life is too short, she says, and family too important, and besides, she reminds us, God has asked us to love.;

Matthew is amazing. He is a big, strong young man but has the heart of a kitten. He is married to a beautiful princess who also became a nurse. It looks like I am going to have plenty of nurses in the family to take care of me when I am old. Matthew and his wife are preparing for the mission field. When he was just five-years old, he told me, "Mama, when I grow up, I am going to be a missionary." Matthew has always known where he was going from the moment he took his first breath in this world. Now and then, this big six foot two man slips and calls me "Mama" like he did when he was little. I just put my arm around his neck and give him a big hug, with my heart bubbling over.

Peter . . . what can I say about Peter? No one I have ever known has had the zeal for life as he has. He is sweet, energetic and lots of fun. He loves to surf, and spend time with his lovely young wife and their two beautiful children. He is an entrepreneur and is working hard at building his own business. Peter is an optimist and believes all things work out for good to those who love the Lord. I think he is right.

Emily is the one my college professor said should never be allowed into existence. I think she would disagree with him. I know I sure do. Emily is my angel girl—she loves Jesus with all her heart and has known since she was a little girl that she would someday become a missionary. She too, like her sister and sister-in-law, became a nurse and headed for Africa two weeks later to work in a health clinic. She is softer spoken and doesn't have that touch of restlessness I sometimes see in her four older siblings, but oh how she loves those four. It seems from the time she was very little, she understood what had happened to them and to me, and in a sense to her too; for when one member of a family suffers, then all the members suffer. Emily has always tried to help us carry that burden.

From the very first moment I found out about my children's abuse, I asked the Lord, "Why did it take so long for me to find out, and where were You when it was going on? I never heard an answer from Him and had to go on, always wondering but never knowing

Then about two years later, I believe the Lord gave me an answer. It was not audibly, but I knew it was Him. I was reminded of a story in the Bible in the book of Daniel where Michael the archangel did battle with the king of Persia, but the help took some time, and Michael did not prevail immediately. I felt the Lord reminding me through that story that abuse had been in the Crawford family for many generations, but not until someone began beseeching the Lord of heaven, could the abuse be revealed and thus stopped. Three years had seemed like an eternity to me, but in the whole picture of perhaps hundreds of years, the interception by God was very swift. "But where were You Lord when they were being abused?" I asked that day. And in the most gentle of ways, I heard Him tell my heart, "I was right there with them every single time—weeping with them and helping them carry the burden. That is how they made it." I then saw a picture of my children when they were being abused, but this time I saw Jesus holding their hands every time abuse took place. I have never asked the Lord those two questions since that day. I believed He gave me the answers. I don't fully understand, but I do trust Him, and I believe Him when He says He will never forsake us.

Someone told me once that children who are believed have the greatest chance for recovery. I don't know how many times I have had grown women come up to me and say, "When I was little, I was being molested, but when I told my mother, she didn't believe me." Well, I believed my children, and I also believe my Lord that He will continue taking them down the road to recovery.

When I was a young mother, I had only two requests I asked from the Lord—one was that all of my children would walk with Him as adults. I didn't care about riches or fame or success. But my prayer was that of the apostle John when he said, "I have no greater joy than to hear that my children walk in truth" (3 John 4). God has granted me that desire … and if I had nothing more in life than that, it would be enough.

But there was one other desire I longed for—a godly husband. After spending so many years raising my children alone and having experienced so much rejection, I really had given up on ever having a husband who loved the Lord and loved me. But just like God so often does in our lives, He showed me His mercy and grace and surprised me one more time—God brought me my troubadour. He came gently into our lives and has never left. He loves the Lord with all his heart, he loves each of my children with a pure, kind love

and most surprisingly of all—he loves me. Sometimes I don't know why. I feel like such a wounded thing, had so many failures, so many miscalculations. And though life has been good to me, there is a scar deep within that changed my life forever. I would have rather died a thousand deaths than to have had my babies abused … and that I must live with all the days of my life.

Subconsciously, I earmark my life with BA and AA: Before Abuse and After Abuse. I think only a mother who has had a child abused can fully understand that. So when my troubadour came along, I didn't know if I could fully love and trust again, but he said, "That's okay—I love you and take you just the way you are. No man has ever said that to me before, no man has ever shown me that kind of love, and it became a perfect picture of the love Jesus Christ has for His bride, the Church. We don't deserve His love, but He gives it to us freely when He becomes Lord of our lives.

Tom Crawford lives in the Midwest, and he is remarried. His father, Ralph, died in 2003 and, as far as I know, went to his grave unrepentant and without having confessed his sins or asking the children for their forgiveness. It is my prayer that Tom will one day tell God and the kids he is sorry … for his own eternal sake and for a further healing to my children's hearts and lives.

If those little flowers wilt and die,
I'll gather them up in my arms
And carry them to the green forest mountains,
Where the river runs freely through.
There, I'll plant them firmly,
In the soil of that little valley
The one which sets between those mountains great.
And sing my psalms for those wee flowers,
Of days gone by, of days to come
And of little flowers, though wilted and gone,
Yet remain in our arms forever.